Physical Characteristics of the Cairn Terrier
(from The Kennel Club breed standard)

BODY
Back level, medium length. Well sprung deep ribs; strong supple loin.

HINDQUARTERS
Very strong muscular thighs. Good, but not excessive, bend of the stifle. Hocks well let down inclining neither in nor out when viewed from the rear.

TAIL
Short, balanced, well furnished with hair but not feathery. Neither high nor low set, carried gaily but not turned down towards back.

COAT
Weather-resistant. Must be double-coated, with profuse, harsh, but not coarse, outer coat; undercoat short, soft and close. Open coats objectionable. Slight wave permissible.

SIZE
Approximately 28-31 cms (11-12 ins) at withers, but in proportion to weight—ideally 6-7.5 kgs (14-16 lbs).

COLOUR
Cream, wheaten, red, grey or nearly black. Brindling in all these colours acceptable. Not solid black, or white, or black and tan. Dark points, such as ears and muzzle, very typical.

FEET
Forefeet larger than hind, may be slightly turned out. Pads thick and strong. Thin, narrow or spreading feet and long nails objectionable.

Cairn Terrier

◇

by Robert Jamieson

Table of Contents

History of the Cairn Terrier — 9
Trace the ancient beginnings of this lively, game and hardy breed; a breed that is certainly 'all terrier!' Follow him from his home in the rugged Scottish Highlands to show rings and pet homes around the world.

Characteristics of the Cairn Terrier — 20
Personality-plus and intelligence in a compact size, the Cairn Terrier is ready for action. Learn about the traits that make the Cairn a wonderful companion, as well as some of the breed's physical characteristics and health considerations.

Breed Standard for the Cairn Terrier — 26
Learn the requirements of a well-bred Cairn Terrier by studying the description of the breed set forth in The Kennel Club standard. Both show dogs and pets must possess key characteristics as outlined in the breed standard.

Your Puppy Cairn Terrier — 32
Be advised about choosing a reputable breeder and selecting a healthy, typical puppy. Understand the responsibilities of ownership, including home preparation, acclimatization, the vet and prevention of common puppy problems.

Everyday Care of Your Cairn Terrier — 62
Enter into a sensible discussion of dietary and feeding considerations, exercise, grooming, travelling and identification of your dog. This chapter discusses Cairn Terrier care for all stages of development.

ISBN 1-902389-34-4

80

PHOTO CREDITS

Photos by Alice van Kempen,

with additional photos by:

Norvia Behling
TJ Calhoun
Carolina Biological Supply
Doskocil
Isabelle Francais
James Hayden-Yoav
James R Hayden, RBP
Bill Jonas

Dwight R Kuhn
Dr Dennis Kunkel
Mikki Pet Products
Phototake
Jean Claude Revy
Dr Andrew Spielman
C James Webb

Illustrations by Renée Low

104

Housebreaking and Training Your Cairn Terrier

by Charlotte Schwartz

Be informed about the importance of training your Cairn Terrier from the basics of housebreaking, and understanding the development of a young dog, to executing obedience commands (sit, stay, down, etc.).

136

Health Care of Your Cairn Terrier

Discover how to select a proper veterinary surgeon and care for your dog at all stages of life. Topics include vaccination scheduling, skin problems, dealing with external and internal parasites and the medical conditions common to the breed.

144

Your Senior Cairn Terrier

Recognise the signs of an ageing dog, both behavioural and medical; implement a senior-care programme with your veterinary surgeon and become comfortable with making the final decisions and arrangements for your senior Cairn Terrier.

Showing Your Cairn Terrier

Experience the dog show world, including different types of shows and the making up of a champion. Go beyond the conformation ring to working trials and agility trials, etc.

Index: **156**

Even though the Cairn Terrier is an ancient breed, it was officially recognised by The Kennel Club in the early 1900s.

HISTORY OF THE
CAIRN TERRIER

The Cairn Terrier is the plucky little dog that hails from the rugged Scottish Highlands. Although this is a game dog with an all-terrier disposition, he is also a loving companion whether he lives in a flat in the city or in a large house in the country.

This book will give you the history, description and the standard of the Cairn Terrier. You will also learn about puppy care, training and the health of the breed. With the colour photographs, you will see that this terrier is cute as a button and a wonderful companion.

This may not be the dog for everyone as terriers are active, busy dogs and this breed is no exception. However, if you like a lively dog, one who will be a devoted family member, this may be the dog for you. And, as is true with most other breeds, once you give your heart and home to a Cairn Terrier, you will remain a devotee to the breed for a lifetime.

HISTORY OF THE BREED
In the history of the dog world, the Cairn Terrier is a fairly ancient breed. However, its official beginnings with The Kennel Club, dating back to the early 1900s, places it as one of the younger recognised terrier breeds. The Cairn Terrier belongs to the group of dogs described as terriers, from the Latin word *terra*, meaning earth. The terrier is a dog that has been bred to work beneath the ground to drive out small and large rodents and

The Cairn's instinctive keenness is well displayed by Dhoran, seen here with Miss Margaret Warner, granddaughter of Lord Borwick who was so influential in the development of the Cairn Terrier.

other animals that can be a nuisance to country living.

All of the dogs in the Terrier Group originated in the British Isles with the exception of the Miniature Schnauzer, whose origins of course trace to Germany. Many of the terrier breeds were derived from a similar ancestor. As recently as the mid-1800s, the terriers fell roughly into two basic categories: the rough-coated, short-legged dogs of Scotland and the longer legged, smooth-coated dogs of England.

The family of Scotch Terriers—those bred in Scotland—divide themselves into the modern Scottish Terrier, the West Highland White Terrier, the Cairn Terrier and the Skye Terrier. In the early 1800s, dogs referred to as Scotch Terriers could be any one of these three breeds. Interbreeding was

> ## Did You Know?
>
> What is a *cairn*? Webster's Dictionary defines *cairn* as a 'heap of stone piled up as a memorial or as a landmark.' Piles of stones in the Highlands marked the graves of the ancient Roman soldiers. In time, brambles, bushes and brush overgrew the rocks and the cairns became ideal places where vermin could make their homes, unseen by man. This was the terrain where the little dog, which was eventually called the Cairn Terrier, plied his skill and earned his name.

common amongst these breeds, and it was not unusual during the 1800s that all three breeds could come from one litter with colour being the deciding factor as to how a particular pup should be classified. J W Benyon wrote in his book *The Cairn Terrier*, 'The Cairn, the West Highland White and the Scottish Terrier were so similar in the early days that the three were inbred with impunity. Early pedigrees of these breeds would show all three breeds in the lineage of a single dog and the three breeds often came from the same litter, sold according to what the buyer wanted.' As breeders started exhibiting at dog shows, it was realised that there must be more uniformity within the breed, i.e. all pups in a litter

The West Highland White Terrier arguably derived from the Cairn Terrier, originally varying only in colour.

In the early years the Cairn was called the Short-haired Skye Terrier and on the mainland he was often called the Tod-hunter. In addition to the Mac Leods, who preferred the dogs of silver-grey colour, other strains of the Cairn were bred by the Mac Donalds of Watermist, who bred dogs of grey and brindle colour, and the Mac Kinnons of Kilbride, who bred the cream, red and dark brindle dogs. All three of these strains form the basis for our present-day Cairn.

The other breed on the Isle of Skye was the Skye Terrier, the long-backed, heavy-bodied dog with the flowing coat. The Skye Terrier breeders did not like it

should look alike as well as being of the same type as their sire and dam.

Much of the early history of the Cairn centres on the Isle of Skye. Take a look at your map of our British Isles and note the remoteness of Skye. It is located to the west of the Highlands and it is part of the Inner Hebrides, a land noted for its rugged typography and tough Scotsmen, where a fearless and tough dog was required to keep the vermin under control. The Cairn, with his large heart and a larger amount of courage, fit the bill for cleaning out vermin in the houses and stables and for clearing the fields and surrounding areas of badgers and foxes. The Cairn history may be a bit convoluted, as the history of many canine breeds is, but it is thought that the oldest strain came from Captain Mac Leod of Drynock on the Isle of Skye.

The Scottish Terrier, one of the four modern-day breeds that derived from the Scotch Terrier family, is a blood relative of the Cairn.

Cairn Terrier

that the newcomer should be called the Short-haired Skye Terrier! An early pioneer and ardent supporter of the breed was Mrs Alastair Campbell, founder of the Brocaire Kennels, who had made frequent trips to the Isle of Skye where she purchased her original dogs. She was the first to enter the breed in a dog show. In 1907, she registered Calla Mhor and Cuillean Bhan as Prick-eared Skye Terriers and entered them in a dog show. Later she registered Rog Mhor, who became the sire of one of the first Challenge Certificate (CC) winners. By 1910, The Kennel Club moved the breed to the classification at dog shows of 'Any other breed or variety' and 24 dogs were registered. The breed was rapidly gaining in popularity even though it still did not have an official name and there was still confusion about which class the dogs should be entered in at dog shows.

In the meantime, the Skye Terrier fancy was still disturbed by the name 'Short-haired Skye Terriers' and protested to The Kennel Club. It was suggested that the breed be called the 'Cairn Terrier of Skye,' which eventually was shortened to Cairn Terrier. Through the efforts of Mrs Campbell, who worked prodigiously on the background of the breed and its breeders, The Kennel Club transferred all Short-haired Skyes to the new registry of Cairn Terriers. In the meantime, in October 1911, an official standard was drawn up for the Cairn at the Scottish Kennel Club Show in Edinburgh as breeders realised that there

Did You Know?

Dr Dieter Fleig in his book *History of Fighting Dogs* wrote, 'Specialists for rat killing in England naturally were dogs with terrier blood in their veins. For this purpose you needed not only a brave dog, which did not shy away from rat bites, but one of truly great speed.'

must be uniformity within the breed. By May 29, 1912, the Cairn Terrier had finally obtained his official status with The Kennel Club and Challenge Certificates were now offered at specific shows.

In addition to the backing of Mrs Alastair Campbell, the breed received early support from Lord Hawke and his sisters Mary and Betty, who had imported terriers from Skye from the Watermist strain. Their dogs, Bridget, Bride and Bruin were 'road markers' in the breed's early history. The first Cairn champion was Gesto, owned by Mrs Campbell.

When World War I started, dog breeding and showing in England basically came to a halt. However, as soon as the war was over, the Cairn's popularity immediately began to rise. New exhibitors joined Mrs Campbell

and by 1923 over 1000 Cairns were registered.

Harviestoun Raider, whelped in 1919 and owned by J E Kerr, became the first great sire of the breed, producing 11 champions, which was a record for the time. Raider stamped his progeny with his wonderful substance, which was sometimes too much for the judges, and passed along all of his best attributes. At the time, Raider was in the background of two-thirds of all Cairn pedigrees.

By the mid-1920s, Mrs N Fleming of Out of the West Kennels was an active breeder and remained so well into the 1930s. Her Fisherman Out of the West and his sire, Doughall Out of the West, were also two important sires throughout the

Many members of the Royal Family were dog lovers and possessed several excellent examples of purebred dogs. Jaggers was amongst the two Cairns. The sketch is by Ernest H Mills.

Did You Know?

Robert Leighton judged the Skye Terriers at Crufts in 1909. He discovered additional classes under the name of 'Short-haired Skyes.' He later wrote, 'Properly speaking, they were not Skye Terriers...but they were certainly interesting. Small, active, game and very hard in appearance, they were strongly though slimly built...and the more I handled them the more I admired them.'

13

In the mid-1930s, Her Royal Highness the Princess Royal had a favourite Cairn named Peggy, which was frequently seen in her company.

breeders found that there was not enough food to keep a kennel running. Some hardy souls did manage to keep a few dogs and, when the war ended, breeding and dog showing resumed as it had after World War I.

In 1943 Splinter produced a son by the name of Sport of Zellah. With the approval of The Kennel Club, the new owner changed his name to Bonfire of Twobees and he was bred in 1948 to Redletter My Choice, owned by Walter Bradshaw. Attention must be given to the Redletter Kennels of Mr Bradshaw because of the huge influence, throughout Great Britain and North America, that the kennel had on the Cairn Terrier. Through the decades, the kennel established a phenomenal record of show wins and top producers.

1920s. In 1933 the great Ch Splinter of Twobees was whelped. The winner of eight Challenge Certificates, he made his mark not in the show ring but with his influence as a sire with his ability to stamp his type and quality onto his get and their next generations. Over 100 champions in England can trace their pedigrees back to him. In addition, he is in the background of many American champions.

Again, with the advent of World War II, dog breeding came to a halt in Great Britain. Many kennels were disbanded when

Did You Know?

The Cairn Terrier, as depicted in paintings from the late 1800s, looks very much like the present-day Cairn. From Mrs Campbell's Calla Mhor to Ch Splinter of Twobees to Ch Cairnwoods Quince, the Cairn Terrier has remained the same in size, structure and coat. This is somewhat unusual, as in many breeds the dog may become significantly larger, or smaller, and there will often be major changes in coat and trimming styles.

Mr Bradshaw started in dogs in the 1920s, raising Flatcoated Retrievers. Shortly before World War II, he became interested in the Cairn Terrier. The breeding of Redletter My Choice to Bonfire Twobees produced Redletter Mc Joe, who became a champion before the age of two years. He was campaigned in the ring for three years and produced nine champions. His son Ch Redletter Mc Murran won 26 Challenge Certificates and was the first Cairn to win an all-breed Best in Show at a Championship Show (1956). His daughter, Ch Redletter Elford Mhorag won 18 CCs. Mc Murran and Mhorag, half-siblings, won both the dog

This historical photo from the 1920s was captioned as follows: 'The selling of puppies in the street is a sight of London. Here every pocket may contain a puppy or something of doggie interest. The salesmen are often fanciers and are allowed to "tell the tale".'

and bitch CCs at five Championship Shows. Ch Redletter Mc Bryan won 17 CCs and sired 13 champions. Ch Redletter Twinlaw Seaspirit, who was the second Cairn to win a Best in Show at a Championship Show, was later purchased by Betty Hyslop of Cairndainia Kennels in Canada. Ch Redletter Marcel won 16 CCs in a single year. Mr Bradshaw died in 1982 at the age of 86, having made up 42 English champions and having had a major impact on the Cairn Terrier world that may not be repeated any time soon.

Other kennels that have made considerable contributions to the Cairn have been: Mrs E H Drummond's Blencathra Kennels,

Kim, the favourite Cairn of Miss Violet Petrie, daughter of Blanche, Lady Petrie (a famed aristocrat of the 1920s), is here seen with its owner.

producers of 25 English champions; the Toptwig Kennels of Mrs Gladys Marsh, which exported dogs to the United States and to Sweden, making an impact in both countries; Mrs H L Manley of Lofthouse Kennels, producing 10 English champions and exporting winning dogs to the US; Oudenarde Kennels, which made up many champions including Am and Can Ch Oudenarde Sea Hark, exported to Betty Hyslop; Uniquecottage Kennels of Mrs J G Parker-Tucker, which produced over 30 English champions who have won many CCs. There have been an exceptional number of dedicated Cairn breeders in the British Isles whose dogs have been well known not only in their own country but also throughout North America.

THE CAIRN IN NORTH AMERICA

The Cairn Terrier's history in America followed the history of the breed in Great Britain by only a few years. In 1913 the first Cairns were imported to the United States by Mrs Henry Price of California from Mrs Fleming's Out of the West Kennels. Sandy Peter Out of the West was the first and only Cairn registered with the American Kennel Club (AKC) in 1913.

By 1917 there were 32 registrations and, by December of that year, the Cairn Terrier Club of America made it as the ninth in the Terrier Group to become a

Cairns of 1835. Here possibly is the ancestor of both the present Cairn and Scottish Terriers, seen at work amongst the rocks after an otter that is attempting to escape. The handwritten inscription reads, 'Scotch terriers at work on a Cairn in the West Highlands.'

imports from Great Britain accounted for two-thirds of the American champions. The Cairn continued his successful and winning ways in America throughout the 1930s and 1940s in spite of the Great Depression and World War II.

Shagbark Kennel of Helen Hunt in Connecticut began in the 1930s and had over 30 champions. In the 1950s Miss Hunt had five generations of homebreds in her kennel. Mrs R T Allen owned the Craigdhu Kennels in Illinois; they were breeders of top Cairns for 45 years. Mrs Betty Stone's Caithness Kennels imported several dogs from England and bred Ch

member of the AKC. Mrs Price became an active breeder and exhibitor through the early 1940s. She had a life-long interest in the breed and served on the board of the national club. Mrs Byron Rogers, a Cairn and Sealyham fancier and also a board member, imported many Cairns from England and wrote the first book on the breed. Mrs C Groverman Ellis of Killybracken Kennels added Cairns to her kennel of Irish Wolfhounds in the 1930s. She produced nearly 40 champions in addition to putting obedience degrees on many of her Cairns. Ch Tam Glen of Killybracken may still be one of the only Cairns with a tracking degree. The owners usually showed their own dogs and purchased few outside dogs, relying upon their homebreds.

Between 1913 and 1930,

A distinguished pair, Mousie and Victory, seen with the Hon Lady Morrison Bell and her daughter, Miss Shelagh Morrison Bell, from the famed family of the 1920s.

Caithness Rufus, who won the Cairn Terrier Club of America national specialty show in 1964 from the puppy class. Rufus sired more than 25 champions and was retired from the show ring to make way for his son, Ch Cairnwoods Golden Boy. Mrs Stone died in the mid-1970s.

Joe and Betty Marcum's, Cairmar Kennels of Mississippi have been very successful, producing Group winners and Best in Show dogs. Two of their dogs, who came from Mrs Stone's Caithness Kennels, were Ch Caithness Barnabas, sire of 31 champions, and Caithness Captie

Did You Know?

The Cairn Terrier and the West Highland White Terrier closely resemble each other. The early Cairn breeders were very careful not to keep Cairn puppies that had any white in their coats; any puppies that did have white were culled at birth. On the other hand, the breeders of the white terriers made certain that their dogs were completely white. Interbreeding of the two breeds continued until 1917 when the American Kennel Club stated that no Cairn could be regis-tered if there was a Westie cross within the first three generations. The Kennel Club followed suit shortly after.

Periwinkle, dam of 7 champions. The Marcums have built their kennel on the strength of their bitches, which proves that 'good producing bitches make a good kennel.' Mrs Marcum is still an active figure in the breed and has written an excellent book on the Cairn Terrier.

The Wolfpit Kennels, started in the 1930s by Mr and Mrs Taylor Coleman and their daughter Lydia Coleman Hutchinson, have produced over 115 champions. Their top winner was Ch Cairnwood's Quince (Ch Cairnwoods Golden Boy ex Caithness Gracenote) who won numerous Groups, an all-breed Best in Show and the national specialty in 1971, 1972, 1973 and again in 1980 at the age of 12. He has been a top-producing sire of the breed, producing over 50 champions. Ch Caithness Rufus was the key dog in his pedigree. Another top stud dog is Ch Caledonian Berry of Wolfpit, winner of many Cairn Terrier specialty shows, 5 all-breed Bests in Show and sire of over 30 champions. Mrs Coleman is a well-known terrier judge in the United States.

One breeder who should be considered a North American breeder rather than a Canadian breeder was Mrs Betty Hyslop of Cairndania Kennels in Ontario, Canada. Mrs Hyslop's influence throughout North America lasted well over sixty years until her death in the late 1990s. She was a well-known figure at the dog shows in both the US and Canada, and the Cairndania dogs were campaigned throughout both countries.

She purchased her first Cairn in 1928 from England and imported and bred dogs through the years, often showing them herself to the top spot. She has thrice won the Terrier Group at Westminster Kennel Club show, America's most prestigious dog show. Every decade has seen great dogs from out of this kennel. Ch Redletter Mc Ruffie won the national specialty three times and sired 25 champions. All-breed Bests in Show were won in the 1960s by Ch Cairndania Mc Brigand's Holbris, Ch Uniquecottage Mr Bradshaw and Ch Cairndania Mc Brigand's Brigery, sire of 27 champions. Ch Redletter Miss Splinters, imported by Mrs Hyslop, was shown 60 times and defeated in the breed only once. The number of Best in Show winners and champions has been considerable, and the North American Cairn fancy was fortunate to have had such a supporter of the breed—one who bred and imported great dogs for so many decades.

In the 1960s Cairns were exported to Japan, France, Sweden, Finland, Australia,

VERE TEMPLE

Denmark and South Africa. Australia and Sweden have been breeding excellent Cairns for many years. You should contact your national kennel club to obtain a list of Cairn Terrier breeders.

The Cairn Terrier, in less than 100 years, has become a very beloved breed. It continues to be in good hands with excellent breeders in Great Britain and America, and the future of the breed is indeed bright.

A special drawing by Vere Temple, which was entitled CAIRN COMPANIONS, came with the following caption: 'These jolly fellows hailing from the North make happy subjects for the artist's pen...and Miss Temple's pen is always skilful.'

19

CHARACTERISTICS OF THE
CAIRN TERRIER

The Cairn Terrier is a wonderful little dog! He's cute, is compact in size, has personality-plus and is an active dog. Some terriers, like the Cairn, are 'below the knee' in height, but in spite of their size, all terriers are masculine dogs and do not show any sign of timidity or shyness. These are busy dogs, on their toes and ready for action!

Have you investigated the responsibilities of owning a Cairn? Or any dog for that matter? This long-haired Dachshund is smaller and usually less active than a Cairn Terrier. Cairns are energetic and always busy.

If you are looking for a sedentary lap dog, this will not be the breed for you.

The Cairn has a very steady disposition and fits in well with family life, whether it be in a large country house or a small flat in the city. He gets along well with children and will accept strangers once he has had a chance to look them over. He's a cocky dog who may not go out and start a fight, but he will surely stand his ground when pushed. This is not a dog who will lay about the house trying to keep his master or mistress happy. He has been bred as a hunter, a dog to go after vermin, and he can be ready to work at the drop of a 'rat.'

Common characteristics of all terriers are their desire to work with great enthusiasm and courage. They all have large and powerful teeth for the size of their bodies; they have keen hearing and excellent eyesight. No matter for how many generations they have been bred, the purpose for which the breed was intended will remain with the dog.

The Cairn Terrier is a versatile dog and a great house dog and companion. If you like to work

Did You Know?

In 1899 Frank Baum wrote *The Emerald City*, later retitled as *The Wonderful Wizard of Oz*. At the turn of the century, Baum's stories were adapted into a popular musical on Broadway. Some years later, the movie musical opened in 1939, with a completely new score by Harold Arlen and the 16-year-old Judy Garland starring as Dorothy. Her dog, Toto, was played by a rather scruffy Cairn Terrier. Dorothy, Toto and the cast of the movie are all still dearly beloved characters in this American classic.

with your dog, you will find the Cairn to be a happy and willing participant in whatever area you choose, be it obedience work, agility, therapy, flyball or, of course, best of all, going-to-ground activities. This is a smart little dog that likes to please, to keep busy and to be challenged. Give him any job that requires a bit of brain activity on his part and he will be a happy camper. Of course, because of his intelligence, it is best to establish very early on who is the head of the household and the very basic obedience lessons are always a good idea. If you are a first-time

You should never buy a dog for its colour alone. If all other desirable characteristics about the puppy are the same (size, temperament, breeding, etc) , then your choice of colour is valid. Some people like dark dogs because they don't show the dirt.

The Cairn is a smart little dog that likes to please. Because of his intelligence, it is best to establish early on who is the head of the household.

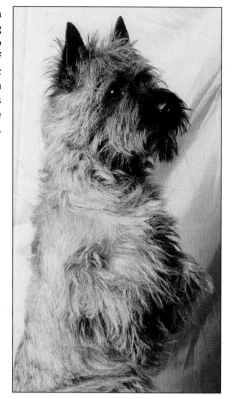

Cairns, as with other terriers, can be a challenge in the obedience ring. Terriers are not easy breeds to work with in obedience as with their intelligence and independent spirit they can sometimes be more trying to train than had been anticipated. You will see Golden Retrievers, Poodles and Border Collies in abundance in obedience classes as these are breeds that are easy to work with. Not only are they intelligent, but more importantly they have a willingness to please their master. The terrier is easily distracted and busy but he is an intelligent dog and he does respond to training. Of course, when training a smart and independent dog, the handler will often learn humility whilst the dog is learning his sits and stays. The Cairn is a quick, alert and intelligent dog and he likes his owner to be his equal.

dog owner, you must be aware of your responsibility toward your new friend. Either keep your dog on a leash or in your fenced garden. Your Cairn, if loose and trotting along your side, will spot a squirrel across a busy street and his instincts will react quickly. Be mindful, for he will dart across the street, never minding the traffic. Therefore, some rudimentary obedience training should be in line so your chum will sit when asked to, come when called and, in general, act like a little gentleman.

Working Trials for Terriers

In the US, The American Working Terrier Association offers a Certificate of Gameness at sanctioned trials. A dog must enter a 10-foot-long tunnel buried in the ground, which includes one right-angle turn. Once in the tunnel, he must reach his prey in 30 seconds. Working trials are held throughout the country and are open to all terriers.

Cairns make great, loving pets, but they should not be allowed to chew on babies' pacifiers, nor should they lick or kiss the baby, for health reasons.

If you plan to become a Cairn Terrier owner you should be aware that this is a breed that will require some grooming. Grooming will be more extensive than with a smooth-coated dog but far less detailed work than with either a Scottish or Bedlington Terrier.

HEALTH CONSIDERATIONS

Cairn Terriers are very healthy dogs, as are most terriers. However, there are health problems in most breeds of dogs and the Cairn Terrier is no exception. The potential and new owner should be aware of these problems. Do remember to buy your puppy from a reputable breeder and ask the breeder if any of these health problems are in her line. It pays to ask questions

Did You Know?

Do you want to live longer? Consider giving a PAT! If you like to volunteer, it is wonderful if you can take your Cairn to a nursing home once a week for several hours. The elder community loves to have a dog to visit with and often your dog will bring a bit of companionship to someone who is either lonely or who may be somewhat detached from the world. You will not only be bringing happiness to someone else but you will also be keeping your little dog busy—and we haven't even mentioned the fact that they have discovered that volunteering helps to increase your longevity!

Cairns are extremely healthy dogs, much healthier, as a rule, than most other dogs. However, you should know about possible illnesses so you can bring the dog to the vet should you have any suspicions of a health problem.

before getting attached to a loveable Cairn baby.

CRANIOMANDIBULAR OSTEOPATHY (CMO)

CMO is a fairly rare disease found in Westies, Scotties and Cairns. It is apparently a hereditary disease although the exact pattern of inheritance is not known. There is a calcification of the joint between the lower jaw and the skull along with a multiplication in growth of bone cells. It usually occurs between four to seven months and it must not be confused with a teething problem or with cancer. Puppies who have this disease will have difficulty in opening their mouths. Diagnosis is made by x-ray and cortisone and homeopathic remedies have been used with good results. This is a very painful disease for the dog.

Did You Know?

For information on the Cairn Terrier in Great Britain and Ireland, the Kennel Club will give you the secretary's name and address for the following clubs:
The Cairn Terrier Club (of England)
The Southern Cairn Terrier Club
The Cairn Terrier Association
The North of Ireland Cairn Terrier Club
Contact the American Kennel Club for the secretary of The Cairn Terrier Club of America.

GLOBOID-CELL LEUKODYSTROPHY (KRABBE'S DISEASE)

Krabbe's disease is inherited as a simple autosomal recessive defect. It is known to be in both the Cairn and the West Highland White Terrier. At about four months of age, the infected dog will show lack of co-ordination and hind leg stiffness. This is a lethal blood disorder and there is no cure or treatment available.

CEREBELLAR HYPOPLASIA

This condition is also passed as a recessive gene, though it is quite unusual and is sometimes reported in cats, related to panleukopenia virus before birth.

Though no conclusive study is available, the condition has been reported in Cairn Terriers.

OTHER CONCERNS

Additionally, hip dysplasia, the most common of orthopaedic problems in dogs, as well as myasthenia gravis, a muscle disorder, inguinal hernias, hemophilia and inhalant allergies have been documented in the breed.

Although these health problems may look daunting, Cairns are considered to be a healthy breed. The problems mentioned are in the breed and a buyer should be aware of them. These diseases are rare and only turn up on the rare occasion. Do not be turned away from the breed but do be aware that if the breeder of your puppy is reputable and aware of these problems, she will be doing her utmost to keep them out of her line.

Williams Haynes wrote in 1925, 'The terrier owner is a "lucky devil" for his dogs do not, as a rule, spend a great deal of time in the hospital. All members of the terrier family, from the giant of the race, the Airedale, way down to little Scottie, owe a big debt to Nature for having blessed them with remarkably robust constitutions. Even when really sick, they make wonderfully rapid recoveries.'

Whilst not all Cairns are obedience and agility performers, all Cairns welcome a game of FETCH with their favourite chew device. Do NOT use a small ball that can be accidentally swallowed.

CAIRN TERRIER

Each breed approved by The Kennel Club has a standard that provides a mental picture of what the specific breed should look like. All reputable breeders strive to produce animals that will meet the requirements of the standard. Many breeds were developed for a specific purpose, i.e. hunting, retrieving, going to ground, coursing, guarding and herding. The terriers were all bred to go to ground and to pursue vermin.

In addition to having dogs that look like proper Cairn Terriers, the standard assures that the Cairn will have the personality, disposition and intelligence that are sought after in the breed.

Standards were originally written by experts who had a love and a concern for the breed. They knew that the essential characteristics of the Cairn Terrier were unlike those of any other breed and that care must be taken that these characteristics were maintained through the generations.

As time progressed and breeders became more aware that certain areas of the dog needed a better description or more definition, breeders would meet together and work out a new standard. However, standards for any breed are never changed on a whim and serious study and exchange between breeders takes place before any move is made. In Britain, The Kennel Club controls the breed standards and any changes or amendments are made by this powerful body.

Did You Know?

The dogs originally known as Scotch terriers include the Cairn, Scottish and Westie. The Scottish Terrier is a heavy-boned, muscular dog whose colours are black, brindle and wheaten. He has a long muzzle and a longer ear compared to the West Highland White or the Cairn Terrier. The Westie is much lighter in weight and bone than the Scottie, he has a shorter, broad muzzle and his ears are smaller than a Scottie's. His colour is white. The Westie is some sturdier than the Cairn, broader in skull and wider in ear carriage. The Cairn has a profuse harsh outer coat with a soft, close undercoat. His coat is shown in a neatened condition rather than in a tailored jacket as are the Scottie and Westie coats.

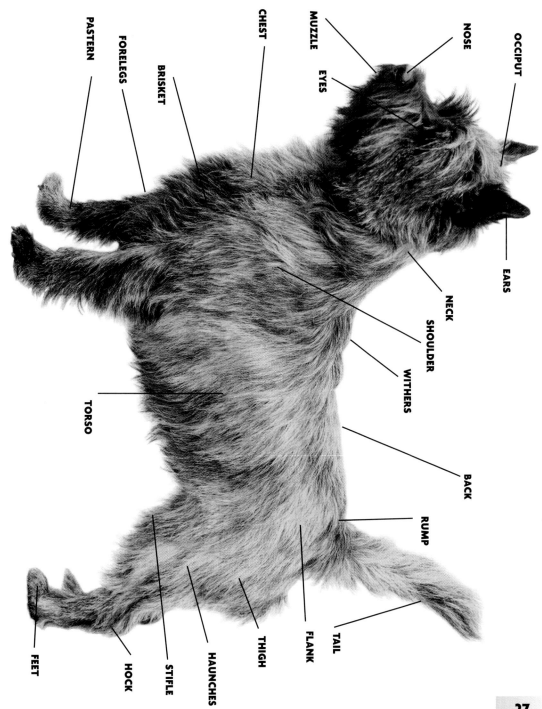

PASTERN

FORELEGS

BRISKET

CHEST

MUZZLE

EYES

NOSE

OCCIPUT

EARS

NECK

SHOULDER

WITHERS

TORSO

BACK

RUMP

FEET

HOCK

STIFLE

HAUNCHES

THIGH

FLANK

TAIL

27

THE KENNEL CLUB STANDARD FOR CAIRN TERRIER

General Appearance: Agile, alert, or workmanlike, natural appearance. Standing well forward on forepaws. Strong quarters. Deep in rib, very free in movement. Weather-resistant coat.

Characteristics: Should impress as being active, game and hardy.

Temperament: Fearless and gay disposition; assertive but not aggressive.

Head and Skull: Head small, but in proportion to body. Skull broad; a decided indentation between the eyes with a definite stop. Muzzle powerful, jaw strong but not long or heavy. Nose black. Head well furnished.

Eyes: Wide apart, medium in size, dark hazel. Slightly sunk with shaggy eyebrows.

Incorrect head and ear set. Head is too thin and ears are too close together.

Ears: Small, pointed, well carried and erect, not too closely set nor heavily coated.

Mouth: Large teeth. Jaws strong with perfect, regular and complete scissor bite, i.e., upper teeth closely overlapping lower teeth and set square to the jaws.

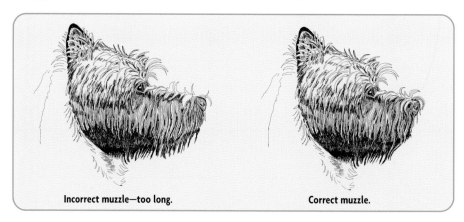

Incorrect muzzle—too long.   Correct muzzle.

Correct head.

Neck: Well set on, not short.

Forequarters: Sloping shoulders, medium length of leg, good but not too heavy bone. Forelegs never out at elbow. Legs covered with harsh hair.

Body: Back level, medium length. Well sprung ribs; strong supple loin.

Hindquarters: Very strong muscular thighs. Good, but not excessive, bend of stifle. Hocks well let down inclining neither in nor out when viewed from the rear.

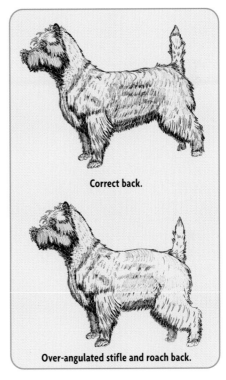

Correct back.

Over-angulated stifle and roach back.

Correct tail.   Incorrect tail due to curl.   Incorrect tail due to high set and feathering.

29

Feet: Forefeet larger than hind, may be slightly turned out. Pads thick and strong. Thin, narrow or spreading feet and long nails objectionable.

Tail: Short, balanced, well furnished with hair but not feathery. Neither high nor low set, carried gaily but not turned down towards back.

Gait/Movement: Very free-flowing stride. Forelegs reaching well forward. Hindlegs giving strong propulsion. Hocks neither too close nor too wide.

Coat: Very important. Weather-resistant. Must be double-coated, with profuse, harsh, but not coarse, outer coat; undercoat short, soft and close. Open coats objectionable. Slight wave permissible.

Colour: Cream, wheaten, red, grey or nearly black. Brindling in all these colours acceptable. Not solid black, or white, or black and tan. Dark points, such as ears and muzzle, very typical.

Size: Approximately 28–31 cms (11–12 ins) at withers, but in proportion to weight: ideally 6–7.5 kgs (14–16 lbs).

Faults: Any departure from the foregoing points should be considered a fault and the seriousness with which the fault should be regarded should be in exact proportion to its degree.

Note: Male animals should have two apparently normal testicles fully descended into the scrotum.

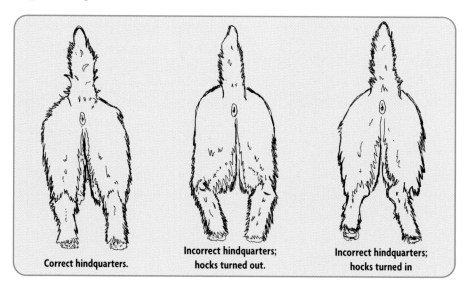

Correct hindquarters.

Incorrect hindquarters; hocks turned out.

Incorrect hindquarters; hocks turned in.

This is what a fine-quality male Cairn Terrier should look like.

CAIRN TERRIER

WHERE TO BEGIN?

If you are convinced that the Cairn Terrier is the ideal dog for you, it's time to learn about where to find a puppy and what to look for. Locating a litter of Cairn Terriers should not present a problem for the new owner. You should enquire about breeders in your area who enjoy a good reputation in the breed. You are looking for an established breeder with outstanding dog ethics and a strong commitment to the breed. New owners should have as many questions as they have doubts. An established breeder is indeed the one to answer your four million questions and make you comfortable with your choice of the Cairn Terrier. An established breeder will sell you a puppy at a fair price if,

A Cairn Terrier and an Irish Wolfhound. The choice between these two breeds is much simpler than choosing between breeds that are closely related like Scottish Terriers, West Highland White Terriers and Skye Terriers, all of whom are closely associated with the development of the Cairn.

and only if, the breeder determines that you are a suitable, worthy owner of his/her dogs. An established breeder can be relied upon for advice, no matter what time of day or night. A reputable breeder will accept a puppy back, without questions, should you decide that this not the right dog for you.

When choosing a breeder, reputation is much more important than convenience of location. Do not be overly impressed by breeders who run brag advertisements in the presses about their stupendous champions and working lines. The real quality breeders are quiet and unassuming. You hear about them at the dog trials and shows, by word of mouth. You may be well advised to avoid the novice who lives only a few miles away. The local novice breeder, trying so hard to get rid of that first litter of puppies, is more than accommodating and anxious to sell you one. That breeder will charge you as much as any established breeder. The novice breeder isn't going to interrogate you and your family about your intentions with the puppy, the environment and training you can

provide, etc. That breeder will be nowhere to be found when your poorly bred, badly adjusted four-pawed monster starts to growl and spit up at midnight or eat the family cat!

Whilst health considerations in the Cairn Terrier are not nearly as daunting as in most other breeds, socialisation is a breeder concern of immense importance. While personality within a breed should be rather consistent, temperament can vary from line to line and socialisation is the first and best way to encourage a proper, stable personality.

Choosing a breeder is an important first step in dog ownership. Fortunately, the majority of Cairn Terrier breeders are devoted to the breed and its well-being. New owners should have little problem finding a reputable breeder who doesn't live

on the other side of the country (or in a different country). The Kennel Club is able to recommend breeders of quality Cairn Terriers, as can any local all-breed club or Cairn Terrier club. Potential owners are encouraged to attend dog shows to see the Cairn Terriers in action, to meet the handlers firsthand and

A male and a female Cairn. The gender of your puppy is a matter of personal taste.

Did You Know?

Unfortunately, when a puppy is bought by someone who does not take into consideration the time and attention that dog ownership requires, it is the puppy who suffers when he is either abandoned or placed in a shelter by a frustrated owner. So all of the 'homework' you do in preparation for your pup's arrival will benefit you both. The more informed you are, the more you will know what to expect and the better equipped you will be to handle the ups and downs of raising a puppy. Hopefully, everyone in the household is willing to do his part in raising and caring for the pup. The anticipation of owning a dog often brings a lot of promises from excited family members: 'I will walk him every day,' 'I will feed him,' 'I will housebreak him,' etc., but these things take time and effort, and promises can easily be forgotten once the novelty of the new pet has worn off.

This Cairn puppy won first prize.

answer questions, recommend breeders and give advice.

Now that you have contacted

to get an idea of what Cairn Terriers look like outside a photographer's lens. Provided you approach the handlers when they are not terribly busy with the dogs, most are more than willing to

At Crufts in 1999, this Cairn took second place in the Terrier Group.

and met a breeder or two and made your choice about which breeder is best suited to your needs, it's time to visit the litter. Keep in mind that many top breeders have waiting lists. Sometimes new owners have to wait as long as two years for a puppy. If you are really committed to the breeder whom you've selected, then you will wait (and hope for an early arrival!). If not, you may have to resort to your second or third choice breeder. Don't be too anxious, however. If the breeder doesn't have any waiting list, or any customers, there is probably a good reason.

Since you are likely to be choosing a Cairn Terrier as a pet dog and not a working dog, you simply should select a pup that is friendly and attractive. Cairn

Did You Know?

Your selection of a good puppy can be determined by your needs. A show potential or a good pet? It is your choice. Every puppy, however, should be of good temperament. Although show-quality puppies are bred and raised with emphasis on physical conformation, responsible breeders strive for equally good temperament. Do not buy from a breeder who concentrates solely on physical beauty at the expense of personality.

Terriers generally have small litters, averaging five puppies, so selection is limited once you have located a desirable litter. While the basic structure of the breed has little variation, the temperament may present trouble in certain strains. Beware of the shy or overly aggressive puppy, be especially conscious of the nervous Cairn Terrier pup. Don't let sentiment or emotion trap you into buying the runt of the litter.

The gender of your puppy is largely a matter of personal taste, especially when choosing a pet, since you will not be breeding the dog. Regardless of gender, all Cairn pups should be lively and alert. In

When visiting a dog show, approach the handlers after they have completed their work in the ring. Many will be happy to talk to you about their breed.

Cairn Terriers, the difference in size is noticeable but slight, males being larger.

Breeders commonly allow visitors to see the litter by around the fifth or sixth week, and puppies leave for their new homes between the eighth and tenth week.

Documentation

Two important documents you will get from the breeder are the pup's pedigree and registration papers. The breeder should register the litter and each pup with The Kennel Club, and it is necessary for you to have the paperwork if you plan on showing or breeding in the future.

Make sure you know the breeder's intentions on which type of registration he will obtain for the pup. There are limited registrations which may prohibit the dog from being shown or from competing in non-conforma-tion trials such as Working or Agility if the breeder feels that the pup is not of sufficient quality to do so. There is also a type of registration that will permit the dog in non-conforma-tion competition only.

If your dog is registered with a Kennel-Club-recognised breed club, then you can register the pup with The Kennel Club yourself. Your breeder can assist you with the specifics of the registration process.

Breeders who permit their puppies to leave early are more interested in your pounds than their puppies' well-being. Puppies need to learn the rules of the trade from their dams, and most dams continue teaching the pups manners and dos and don'ts until around the eighth week. Breeders spend significant amounts of time with the Cairn Terrier toddlers so that they are able to interact with the 'other species', i.e. humans. Given the long history that dogs and humans have, bonding between the two species is natural but must be nurtured. A well-bred, well-socialised Cairn Terrier pup wants nothing more than to be near you and please you.

Always check the bite of your selected puppy to be sure that it is neither overshot or undershot. This may not be too noticeable on a young puppy but it is still important to check for overall soundness.

COMMITMENT OF OWNERSHIP
After considering all of these factors, you have most likely already made some very important decisions about selecting your puppy. You have chosen a Cairn Terrier, which means that you have decided which characteristics you want in a dog and what type of dog will best fit into your family and

Visiting a sleeping litter won't do much good when choosing a pup. You must observe the dynamics of the 'pack' and learn about each pup's individual personality, then choose the one that best suits you.

Insurance

Many good breeders will offer you insurance with your new puppy, which is an excellent idea. The first few weeks of insurance will probably be covered free of charge or with only minimal cost, allowing you to take up the policy when this expires. If you own a pet dog, it is sensible to take out such a policy as veterinary fees can be high, although routine vaccinations and boosters are not covered. Look carefully at the many options open to you before deciding which suits you best.

Are You a Fit Owner?

If the breeder from whom you are buying a puppy asks you a lot of personal questions, do not be insulted. Such a breeder wants to be sure that you will be a fit provider for his puppy.

Observing pups will help you to learn to recognise certain behaviour. By the third or fourth week, the pups' personalities begin to emerge.

lifestyle. If you have selected a breeder, you have gone a step further—you have done your research and found a responsible, conscientious person who breeds quality Cairn Terrier and who should be a reliable source of help as you and your puppy adjust to life together. If you have observed a litter in action, you have obtained a firsthand look at the dynamics of a puppy 'pack' and, thus, you should learn about each pup's individual personality—perhaps you have even found one that particularly appeals to you.

However, even if you have not yet found the Cairn Terrier puppy of your dreams, observing pups will help you learn to recognise certain behaviour and to determine what a pup's behaviour indicates about his temperament. You will be able to pick out which pups are the leaders, which ones are less

At four weeks of age, the puppies are still too young to be removed from their mother. Potential owners are well advised to meet the dam of the litter to evaluate her personality and temperament.

outgoing, which ones are confident, which ones are shy, playful, friendly, aggressive, etc. Equally as important, you will learn to recognise what a healthy pup should look and act like. All of these things will help you in your search, and when you find the Cairn Terrier that was meant for you, you will know it!

Researching your breed, selecting a responsible breeder and observing as many pups as possible are all important steps on the way to dog ownership. It may seem like a lot of effort…and you have not even brought the pup home yet!

Your Schedule . . .

If you lead an erratic, unpredictable life, with daily or weekly changes in your work requirements, consider the problems of owning a puppy. The new puppy has to be fed regularly, socialised (loved, petted, handled, introduced to other people) and, most importantly, allowed to visit outdoors for toilet training. As the dog gets older, it can be more tolerant of deviations in its feeding and toilet relief.

39

Cairn Terrier

As adorable as a teddy, your Cairn still requires supervision. Cairns can tear stuffed animals apart in very short order, perhaps swallowing bits that may cause serious health problems. Only use toys made especially for dogs.

Remember, though, you cannot be too careful when it comes to deciding on the type of dog you want and finding out about your prospective pup's background. Buying a puppy is not—or should not be—just another whimsical purchase. This is one instance in which you actually do get to choose your own family! You may be thinking that buying a puppy should be fun—it should not be so serious and so much work. Keep in mind that your puppy is not a cuddly stuffed toy or decorative lawn ornament, but a creature that will become a real member of your family. You will come to realise that, whilst buying a puppy is a pleasurable and exciting endeavour, it is not something to be taken lightly. Relax…the fun will start when the pup comes home!

Always keep in mind that a puppy is nothing more than a baby in a furry disguise…a baby who is virtually helpless in a human world and who trusts his owner for fulfilment of his basic needs for survival. In addition to water and shelter, your pup needs care, protection, guidance and love. If you are not prepared to commit to this, then you are not prepared to own a dog.

Wait a minute, you say. How hard could this be? All of my neighbours own dogs and they seem to be doing just fine. Why should I have to worry about all of this? Well, you should not worry about it; in fact, you will probably find that once your Cairn Terrier pup gets used to his new home, he will fall into his place in the family quite naturally. But it never hurts to emphasise the commitment of dog ownership. With some time and patience, it is really not too difficult to raise a curious and exuberant Cairn Terrier pup to be a well-adjusted and well-mannered adult dog—a dog that could be your most loyal friend.

Did You Know?

The cost of food must also be mentioned. All dogs need a good quality food with an adequate supply of protein to develop their bones and muscles properly. Most dogs are not picky eaters but unless fed properly they can quickly succumb to skin problems.

PREPARING PUPPY'S PLACE

Researching your breed and finding a breeder are only two aspects of the 'homework' you will have to do before bringing your Cairn Terrier puppy home. You will also have to prepare your home and family for the new addition. Much as you would prepare a nursery for a newborn baby, you will need to designate a place in your home that will be the puppy's own. How you prepare your home will depend on how much freedom the dog will be allowed. Whatever you decide, you must ensure that he has a place that he can 'call his own.'

When you bring your new puppy into your home, you are bringing him into what will become his home as well. Obviously, you did not buy a puppy so that he could take over your house, but in order for a puppy to grow into a stable, well-adjusted dog, he has to feel comfortable in his surroundings. Remember, he is leaving the warmth and security of his mother and littermates, as well as the familiarity of the only place he has ever known, so it is important to make his transition as easy as possible. By preparing a place in your home for the puppy, you are making him feel as welcome as possible in a strange new place. It should not take him long to get used to it, but the sudden shock of being transplanted is somewhat traumatic for a young pup. Imagine

how a small child would feel in the same situation—that is how your puppy must be feeling. It is up to you to reassure him and to let him know, 'Little fellow, you are going to like it here!'

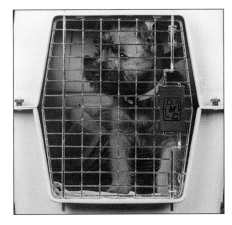

This small-size crate is sufficient for a puppy or a fully grown Cairn Terrier. Once acclimated, your dog will be perfectly happy and secure in his crate.

WHAT YOU SHOULD BUY

CRATE

To someone unfamiliar with the use of crates in dog training, it may seem like punishment to shut a dog in a crate, but this is not the case at all. Although all breeders do not advocate crate training, more and more breeders and trainers are recommending crates as a preferred tool for show puppies as well as pet puppies. Crates are not cruel—crates have many humane and highly effective uses in dog care and training. For example, crate training is a very popular and very successful housebreaking method. A crate can keep your dog safe during travel and, perhaps most

PHOTO COURTESY OF DISKOCIL

cosy pseudo-den for your dog. Like his ancestors, he too will seek out the comfort and retreat of a den—you just happen to be providing him with something a little more luxurious than his early ancestors enjoyed.

As far as purchasing a crate, the type that you buy is up to you. It will most likely be one of the two most popular types: wire or fibreglass. There are advantages and disadvantages to each type. For example, a wire crate is more open, allowing the air to flow through and affording the dog a view of what is going on around him whilst a fibreglass crate is sturdier. Both can double as travel crates, providing protection for the dog. The size of the crate is another thing to consider. A small crate will be fine for a Cairn Terrier pup or adult.

BEDDING
Veterinary bedding in the dog's crate will help the dog feel more at home and you may also like to pop in a small blanket. This will take the place of the leaves, twigs, etc., that the pup would use in the wild to make a den; the pup can make his own 'burrow' in the crate. Although your pup is far removed from his den-making ancestors, the denning instinct is still a part of his genetic makeup. Second, until you bring your pup home, he has been sleeping amidst the warmth of his mother and

Your local pet shop offers a variety of crates from which to choose. The mid-size crate is desirable for the Cairn.

importantly, a crate provides your dog with a place of his own in your home. It serves as a 'doggie bedroom' of sorts—your Cairn Terrier can curl up in his crate when he wants to sleep or when he just needs a break. Many dogs sleep in their crates overnight. When lined with soft bedding and a favourite toy, a crate becomes a littermates, and whilst a blanket is not the same as a warm, breathing body, it still provides heat and something with which to snuggle. You will want to wash your pup's bedding frequently in case he has an accident in his crate, and replace or remove any blanket that becomes ragged and starts to fall apart.

Toys

Toys are a must for dogs of all ages, especially for curious playful

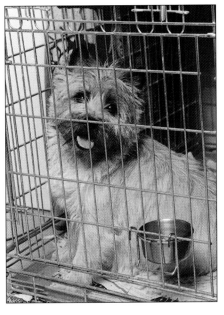

Wire crates are popular for use in the home. These crates provide better ventilation and visibility for your Cairn.

Did You Know?

During crate training, you should partition off the section of the crate in which the pup stays. If he is given too big an area, this will hinder your training efforts. Crate training is based on the fact that a dog does not like to soil his sleeping quarters, so it is ineffective to keep a pup in a crate that is so big that he can eliminate in one end and get far enough away from it to sleep. Also, you want to make the crate den-like for the pup. Blankets and a favourite toy will make the crate cosy for the small pup; as he grows, you may want to evict some of his 'roommates' to make more room.

It will take some coaxing at first, but be patient. Given some time to get used to it, your pup will adapt to his new home-within-a-home quite nicely.

pups. Puppies are the 'children' of the dog world, and what child does not love toys? Chew toys provide enjoyment to both dog and owner—your dog will enjoy playing with his favourite toys, whilst you will enjoy the fact that they distract him from your expensive shoes and leather sofa. Puppies love to chew; in fact, chewing is a physical need for pups as they are teething, and everything looks appetising! The full range of your possessions— from old dishcloth to Oriental rug—are fair game in the eyes of a teething pup. Puppies are not all that discerning when it comes to finding something to literally 'sink their teeth into'—everything tastes great!

Safe and popular knotted tugs are effective as pacifiers and dental devices.

Pet shops offer dog toys that have been approved for their tear-resistance. Never offer a Cairn Terrier human toys that can be readily destroyed and swallowed.

Toys, Toys, Toys!

With a big variety of dog toys available, and so many that look like they would be a lot of fun for a dog, be careful in your selection. It is amazing what a set of puppy teeth can do to an innocent-looking toy, so, obviously, safety is a major consideration. Be sure to choose the most durable products that you can find. Hard nylon bones and toys are a safe bet, and many of them are offered in different scents and flavours that will be sure to capture your dog's attention. It is always fun to play a game of catch with your dog, and there are balls and flying discs that are specially made to withstand dog teeth.

Squeaky toys are quite popular, but must be avoided for the Cairn Terrier. Perhaps a squeaky toy can be used as an aid in training, but not for free play. If a pup 'disembowels' one of these, the small plastic squeaker inside can be dangerous if swallowed. Monitor the condition of all your pup's toys carefully and get rid of any that have been chewed to the point of becoming potentially dangerous.

Be careful of natural bones, which have a tendency to splinter into sharp, dangerous pieces. Also be careful of rawhide, which can turn into pieces that are easy to swallow or into a mushy mess on your carpet.

If you want your dog to be near you during certain parts of the day or night, get him an easily movable bed and place it close to where you are sitting.

LEAD

A nylon lead is probably the best option as it is the most resistant to puppy teeth should your pup take a liking to chewing on his lead. Of course, this is a habit that should be nipped in the bud, but if your pup likes to chew on his lead he has a very slim chance of being able to chew through the strong nylon. Nylon leads are also lightweight, which is good for a young Cairn Terrier who is just getting used to the idea of walking on a lead. For everyday walking and safety purposes, the nylon lead is a good choice. As your pup grows up and gets used to walking on the lead, you may want to purchase a flexible lead. These leads allow you to extend the length to give the dog a broader area to explore or to shorten the length to keep the close to you. Of course there are special leads for training purposes, but these are not

A leash or lead is not a chew toy, and your Cairn has to learn that chewing on the leash is unacceptable behaviour.

Your local pet shop will have a wide selection of leashes from which you can make a choice.

Financial Responsibility

Grooming tools, collars, leashes, dog beds and, of course, toys will be an expense to you when you first obtain your pup, and the cost will trickle on throughout your dog's lifetime. If your puppy damages or destroys your possessions (as most puppies surely will!) or something belonging to a neighbour, you can calculate additional expense. There is also flea and pest control, which every dog owner faces more than once. You must be able to handle the financial responsibility of owning a dog.

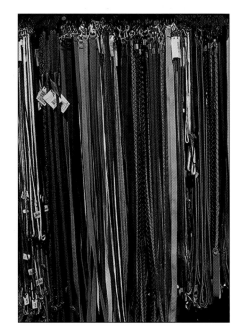

necessary for routine walks with your Cairn Terrier.

COLLAR

Your pup should get used to wearing a collar all the time since you will want to attach his ID tags to it. Plus, you have to attach the lead to something! A lightweight nylon collar is a good choice; make sure that it fits snugly enough so that the pup cannot wriggle out of it, but is loose enough so that it will not be uncomfortably tight around the pup's neck. You should be able to fit a finger between the pup and the collar. It may take some time for your pup to get used to wearing the collar, but soon he will not even notice that it is there. Choke collars are made for training, but should only be used by an experienced handler.

FOOD AND WATER BOWLS

Your pup will need two bowls, one for food and one for water. You may want two sets of bowls, one for inside and one for outside, depending on where the dog will be fed and where he will be spending most of his time. Stainless steel or sturdy plastic bowls are popular choices. Plastic bowls are more chewable. Dogs tend not to chew on the steel variety, which can be sterilised. It is important to buy sturdy bowls since anything is in danger of being chewed by puppy teeth and you do not want your dog to be constantly

Stainless steel bowls for water or food, as well as heavy pottery bowls, are available for Cairns that tend to chew up the plastic bowls.

chewing apart his bowl (for his safety and for your purse!).

CLEANING SUPPLIES

Until a pup is housetrained you will be doing a lot of cleaning. Accidents will occur, which is okay in the beginning because the puppy does not know any better. All you can do is be prepared to clean up any 'accidents.' Old rags, towels, newspapers and a safe disinfectant are good to have on hand.

BEYOND THE BASICS

The items previously discussed are the bare necessities. You will find out what else you need as you go along—grooming supplies, flea/tick protection, baby gates to partition a

The Cairn puppy should become accustomed to wearing a collar at all times. Be sure that his identification tags are securely fastened.

47

Your local pet shop sells an array of dishes and bowls for water and food.

It is your responsibility to clean up after your dog has relieved himself. Pet shops have various tools to assist in the cleanup job.

PHOTO COURTESY OF MIKKI PET PRODUCTS.

room, etc. These things will vary depending on your situation but it is important that you have everything you need to feed and make your Cairn Terrier comfortable in his first few days at home.

PUPPY-PROOFING YOUR HOME

Aside from making sure that your Cairn Terrier will be comfortable in your home, you also have to make sure that your home is safe for your Cairn Terrier. This means taking precautions that your pup will not get into anything he should not get into and that there is nothing within his reach that may harm him should he sniff it, chew it, inspect it, etc. This probably seems obvious since, whilst you

The BUCKLE COLLAR is the standard collar used for everyday purpose. Be sure that you adjust the buckle on growing puppies. Check it every day. It can become too tight overnight! These collars can be made of leather or nylon. Attach your dog's identification tags to this collar.

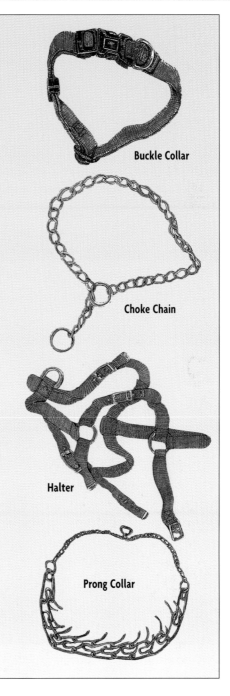

Buckle Collar

The CHOKE CHAIN is the usual collar recommended for training. It is constructed of highly polished steel so that it slides easily through the stainless steel loop. The idea is that the dog controls the pressure around its neck and he will stop pulling if the collar becomes uncomfortable. Never leave a choke collar on your dog when not training.

Choke Chain

The HALTER is for a trained dog that has to be restrained to prevent running away, chasing a cat and the like. Considered the most humane of all collars, it is frequently used on smaller dogs for which collars are not comfortable.

Halter

The PRONG COLLAR certainly appears ominous, like an ancient instrument of torture. This collar is forbidden in Britain because it could easily harm a dog. More humane training devices are recommended for all owners.

Prong Collar

Chemical Toxins

Scour your carport for potential puppy dangers. Remove weed killers, pesticides and antifreeze materials. Antifreeze is highly toxic and even a few drops can kill an adult dog. The sweet taste attracts the animal, who will quickly consume it from the floor or curbside.

are primarily concerned with your pup's safety, at the same time you do not want your belongings to be ruined. Breakables should be placed out of reach if your dog is to have full run of the house. If he is to be limited to certain places within the house, keep any potentially dangerous items in the 'off-limits' areas. An electrical cord can pose a danger should the puppy decide to taste it—and who is going to convince a pup that it would not

Puppy-Proofing

Thoroughly puppy-proof your house before bringing your puppy home. Never use roach or rodent poisons in any area accessible to the puppy. Avoid the use of toilet bowl cleaners. Most dogs are born with toilet bowl sonar and will take a drink if the lid is left open. Also keep the rubbish secured and out of reach.

make a great chew toy? Cords should be fastened tightly against the wall. If your dog is going to spend time in a crate, make sure that there is nothing near his crate that he can reach if he sticks his curious little nose or paws through the openings. Just as you would with a child, keep all household cleaners and chemicals where the pup cannot get to them.

It is also important to make sure that the outside of your home is safe. Of course your puppy should never be unsupervised, but a pup let loose in the garden will want to run and explore, and he should be granted that freedom. Do not let a fence give you a false sense of security; you would be surprised how crafty (and persistent) a dog can be in working out how to dig under and squeeze his way through small holes, or to jump or climb over a fence. The remedy is to make the fence high enough so that it really is impossible for your dog to get over it (about 3 metres should suffice), and well embedded into the ground. Be sure to repair or secure any gaps in the fence. Check the fence periodically to ensure that it is in good shape and make repairs as needed—a very determined pup, especially an 'earth dog' like your Cairn Terrier, may return to the same spot to 'work on it' until he is able to get through.

FIRST TRIP TO THE VET

You have picked out your puppy, and your home and family are ready. Now all you have to do is collect your Cairn Terrier from the breeder and the fun begins, right? Well…not so fast. Something else you need to prepare is your pup's first trip to the veterinary surgeon. Perhaps the breeder can recommend someone in the area that specialises in Cairn Terriers, or maybe you know some other Cairn Terrier owners who can suggest a good vet. Either way, you should have an appointment arranged for your pup before you pick him up and plan on taking him for an examination before bringing him home.

The pup's first visit will consist of an overall examination to make sure that the pup does not have any problems that are not apparent to the eye. The veterinary surgeon will also set up a schedule for the pup's vaccinations; the breeder will inform you of which ones the pup has already received and the vet can continue from there.

INTRODUCTION TO THE FAMILY

Everyone in the house will be excited about the puppy coming home and will want to pet him and play with him, but it is best to make the introduction low-key so as not to overwhelm the puppy. He is apprehensive already. It is the first time he has been separated from his mother and the breeder,

Sturdy chew toys are entertaining, healthful diversions for your Cairn puppy. This will keep your new puppy from chewing on forbidden objects, such as electrical cords.

and the ride to your home is likely the first time he has been in a car. The last thing you want to do is smother him, as this will only frighten him further. This is not to say that human contact is not extremely necessary at this stage, because this is the time when a connection between the pup and his human family is formed. Gentle petting and soothing words should help console him, as well as just putting him down and letting him explore on his own (under your watchful eye, of course).

The pup may approach the family members or may busy

Natural Toxins

Examine your lawn and garden landscaping before bringing your puppy home. Many varieties of plants have leaves, stems or flowers that are toxic if ingested, and you can depend on a curious puppy to investigate them. Ask your veterinarian for information on poisonous plants or research them at your library.

Removing the puppy from his mother and taking him to your home requires a definite 'getting-to-know you' ritual of soothing words and soft touches. It is hard to be a substitute for any dog's mother, but that's what you have to be.

Did You Know?

It will take at least two weeks for your puppy to become accustomed to his new surroundings. Give him lots of love, attention, handling, frequent opportunities to relieve himself, a diet he likes to eat and a place he can call his own.

himself with exploring for a while. Gradually, each person should spend some time with the pup, one at a time, crouching down to get as close to the pup's level as possible and letting him sniff their hands and petting him gently. He definitely needs human attention and he needs to be touched—this is

Did You Know?

Taking your dog from the breeder to your home in a car can be a very uncomfortable experience for both of you. The puppy will have been taken from his warm, friendly, safe environment and brought into a strange new environment. An environment that moves! Be prepared for loose bowels, urination, crying, whining and even fear biting. With proper love and encouragement when you arrive home, the stress of the trip should quickly disappear.

how to form an immediate bond. Just remember that the pup is experiencing a lot of things for the first time, at the same time. There are new people, new noises, new smells, and new things to investigate: so be gentle, be affectionate, and be as comforting as you can be.

YOUR PUP'S FIRST NIGHT HOME

You have travelled home with your new charge safely in his basket or crate. He's been to the vet for a thorough check-up, he's been weighed, his papers examined; perhaps he's even been vaccinated and wormed as well. He's met the family, licked the whole family, including the excited children and the less-than-happy cat. He's explored his area, his new bed, the garden and anywhere else he's been permitted. He's eaten his first meal at home and relieved himself in the proper place. He's heard lots of new sounds, smelled new friends and seen more of the outside world than ever before.

That was just the first day! He's worn out and is ready for bed…or so you think!

It's puppy's first night and you are ready to say 'Good night'—keep in mind that this is puppy's first night ever to be sleeping alone. His dam and littermates are no longer at paw's length and he's a bit scared, cold and lonely. Be reassuring to your new family member. This is not the time to spoil him and give in to his inevitable whining.

Puppies whine. They whine to let the others know where they are and hopefully to get company out of it. Place your pup in his new bed or crate in his room and close the door. Mercifully, he may fall asleep without a peep. If the inevitable occurs, ignore the whining: he is fine. Be strong and keep his interest in mind. Do not allow your heart to become guilty and visit the pup. He will fall asleep.

Many breeders recommend placing a piece of bedding from his former home in his new bed so that he recognises the scent of his litter-mates. Others still advise placing a hot water bottle in his bed for warmth. This latter may be a good idea provided the pup doesn't attempt to suckle—he'll get good and wet and may not fall asleep so fast.

Puppy's first night can be somewhat stressful for the pup and his new family. Remember that you

are setting the tone of nighttime at your house. Unless you want to play with your pup every evening at 10 p.m., midnight and 2 a.m., don't initiate the habit. Your family will thank you, and so will your pup!

When a child and a Cairn grow up together, there is an unmistakable bond that develops between them.

Did You Know?

You will probably start feeding your pup the same food that he has been getting from the breeder; the breeder should give you a few days' supply to start you off. Although you should not give your pup too many treats, you will want to have puppy treats on hand for coaxing, training, rewards, etc. Be careful, though, as a small pup's calorie requirements are relatively low and a few treats can add up to almost a full day's worth of calories without the required nutrition.

Cairns are friendly, intelligent dogs. Some of their best friends can be cats! It all depends upon a process called socialisation.

PREVENTING PUPPY PROBLEMS

SOCIALISATION

Now that you have done all of the preparatory work and have helped your pup get accustomed to his new home and family, it is about time for you to have some fun!

Socialisation

Thorough socialisation includes not only meeting new people but also being introduced to new experiences such as riding in the auto, having his coat brushed, hearing the television, walking in a crowd—the list is endless. The more your pup experiences, and the more positive the experiences are, the less of a shock and the less scary it will be for your pup to encounter new things.

Socialising your Cairn Terrier pup gives you the opportunity to show off your new friend, and your pup gets to reap the benefits of being an adorable furry creature that people will want to pet and, in general, think is absolutely precious!

Besides getting to know his new family, your puppy should be exposed to other people, animals and situations, but of course he must not come into close contact with dogs you don't know well until his course of injections is fully complete. This will help him become well adjusted as he grows up and less prone to being timid or fearful of the new things he will encounter. Your pup's socialisation began at the breeder's but now it is your responsibility to continue it. The socialisation he receives up until the age of 12 weeks is the most critical, as this is the time when he forms his impressions of the outside world. Be especially careful during the eight-to-ten-week period, also known as the fear period. The interaction he receives during this time should be gentle and reassuring. Lack of socialisation can manifest itself in fear and aggression as the dog grows up. He needs lots of human contact, affection, handling and exposure to other animals.

Once your pup has received his necessary vaccinations, feel free to take him out and about (on his lead, of course). Walk him around the neighbourhood, take him on your daily errands, let people pet

Your Cairn not only has to be socialised with humans but he has to get along with other dogs as well.

When you first bring your Cairn puppy home, he only has the imprint of family life with his own mother. You are responsible for the behaviour and understanding through which your Cairn can exist in the human world.

him, let him meet other dogs and pets, etc. Puppies do not have to try to make friends; there will be no shortage of people who will want to introduce themselves. Just make sure that you carefully supervise each meeting. If the neighbourhood children want to say hello, for example, that is great—children and pups most often make great companions. Sometimes an excited child can unintentionally handle a pup too roughly, or an overzealous pup can playfully nip a little too hard. You want to make socialisation experiences positive ones. What a pup learns during this very formative stage will impact his attitude toward future encounters. You want your dog to be comfortable around everyone. A pup that has a bad experience with a child may grow up to be a dog that is shy around or aggressive toward children.

Boy or Girl?

An important consideration to be discussed is the sex of your puppy. For a family companion, a bitch may be the better choice, considering the female's inbred concern for all young creatures and her accompanying tolerance and patience. It is always advised to spay a pet bitch, which may guarantee her a longer life.

CONSISTENCY IN TRAINING

Dogs, being pack animals, naturally need a leader, or else they try to establish dominance in their packs. When you bring a dog into your family, the choice of who becomes the leader and who becomes the 'pack' is entirely up to you! Your

Cairns, like other terriers, are dog-aggressive. If properly socialised with other dogs, your Cairn will accept other dogs when introduced on neutral ground.

Training Tip

Training your puppy takes much patience and can be frustrating at times, but you should see results from your efforts. If you have a puppy that seems untrainable, take him to a trainer or behaviourist. The dog may have a personality problem that requires the help of a professional, or perhaps you need help in learning how to train your dog.

No Chocolate

Use treats to bribe your dog into a desired behaviour. Try small pieces of hard cheese or freeze-dried liver. Never offer chocolate as it has toxic qualities for dogs.

Natural Toxins

Examine your lawn and garden landscaping before bringing your puppy home. Many varieties of plants have leaves, stems or flowers that are toxic if ingested, and you can depend on a curious puppy to investigate them. Ask your veterinarian for information on poisonous plants or research them at your library.

pup's intuitive quest for dominance, coupled with the fact that it is nearly impossible to look at an adorable Cairn Terrier pup, with his 'puppy-dog' eyes and his too-big-for-his-head ears, and not cave in, give the pup almost an

Toxic Plants

Many plants can be toxic to dogs. If you see your dog carrying a piece of vegetation in his mouth, approach him in a

quiet, disinterested manner, avoid eye contact, pet him and gradually remove the plant from his mouth. Alternatively, offer him a treat and maybe he'll drop the plant on his own accord. Be sure no toxic plants are growing in your own garden.

unfair advantage in getting the upper hand! A pup will definitely test the waters to see what he can and cannot do. Do not give in to those pleading eyes—stand your ground when it comes to disciplining the pup and make sure that all family members do the same. It will only confuse the pup when Mother tells him to get off the couch when he is used to sitting up there with Father to watch the nightly news. Avoid discrepancies by having all members of the household decide on the rules before the pup even comes home…and be consistent in enforcing them! Early training shapes the dog's personality, so you cannot be unclear in what you expect.

COMMON PUPPY PROBLEMS
The best way to prevent puppy problems is to be proactive in stopping an undesirable

behaviour as soon as it starts. The old saying 'You can't teach an old dog new tricks' does not necessarily hold true, but it is true that it is much easier to discourage bad behaviour in a young developing pup than to wait until the pup's bad behaviour becomes the adult dog's bad habit. There are some problems that are especially prevalent in puppies as they develop.

NIPPING

As puppies start to teethe, they feel the need to sink their teeth into anything available...unfortunately that includes your fingers, arms, hair and toes. You may find this behaviour cute for the first five seconds...until you feel just how sharp those puppy teeth are. This is something you want to discourage immediately and consistently with a firm 'No!' (or whatever number of firm 'No's' it takes for him to understand that you mean business). Then replace your finger with an appropriate chew toy. Whilst this behaviour is merely annoying when the dog is young, it can become dangerous as your Cairn Terrier's adult teeth grow in and his jaws develop, and he continues to think it is okay to gnaw on human appendages. Your Cairn Terrier does not mean any harm with a friendly nip, but even a small dog can have a big bite if he doesn't know any better.

Chewing Tips

Chewing goes hand in hand with nipping in the sense that a teething puppy is always looking for a way to soothe his aching gums. In this case, instead of chewing on you, he may have taken a liking to your favourite shoe or something else which he should not be chewing. Again, realise that this is a normal canine behaviour that does not need to be discouraged, only redirected. Your pup just needs to be taught what is acceptable to chew on and what is off limits. Consistently tell him NO when you catch him chewing on something forbidden and give him a chew toy. Conversely, praise him when you catch him chewing on something appropriate. In this way you are discouraging the inappropriate behaviour and reinforcing the desired behaviour. The puppy chewing should stop after his adult teeth have come in, but an adult dog continues to chew for various reasons—perhaps because he is bored, perhaps to relieve tension or perhaps he just likes to chew. That is why it is important to redirect his chewing when he is still young.

CRYING/WHINING

Your pup will often cry, whine, whimper, howl or make some type of commotion when he is left

59

house and he cannot see you. The noise he is making is an expression of the anxiety he feels at being alone, so he needs to be taught that being alone is okay. You are not actually training the dog to stop making noise, you are training him to feel comfortable when he is alone and thus removing the need for him to make the noise. This is where the crate filled with cosy bedding and a toy comes in handy. You want to know that he is safe when you are not there to supervise, and you know that he will be safe in his crate rather than roaming freely about the house. In order for the pup to stay in his crate without making a fuss, he needs to be comfortable in his crate. On that note, it is extremely important that the crate is never used as a form of punishment, or the pup will have a negative association with the crate.

The majority of problems that

alone. This is basically his way of calling out for attention to make sure that you know he is there and that you have not forgotten about him. He feels insecure when he is left alone, when you are out of the house and he is in his crate or when you are in another part of the

Did You Know?

Some experts in canine health advise that stress during a dog's early years of development can compromise and weaken his immune system and may trigger the potential for a shortened life expectancy. They emphasize the need for happy and stress-free growing-up years.

are commonly seen in young pups will disappear as your dog gets older. However, how you deal with problems when he is young will determine how he reacts to discipline as an adult dog. It is important to establish who is boss (hopefully it will be you!) right away when you are first bonding with your dog. This bond will set the tone for the rest of your life together. Accustom the pup to the crate in short, gradually increasing time intervals in which you put him in the crate, maybe with a treat, and stay in the room with him. If he cries or makes a fuss, do not go to him, but stay in his sight. Gradually he will realise that staying in his crate is all right without your help, and it will not be so traumatic for him when you are not around. You may want to leave the radio on softly when you leave the house; the sound of human voices may be comforting to him.

Natural Toxins

The majority of problems that is commonly seen in young pups will disappear as your dog gets older. However, how you deal with problems when he is young will determine how he reacts to discipline as an adult dog. It is important to establish who is boss (hopefully it will be you!) right away when you are first bonding with your dog. This bond will set the tone for the rest of your life together.

Your Cairn will accept his crate as a safe haven and not feel lonely when he is placed in it. This is key to preventing separation anxiety in young pups.

DIETARY AND FEEDING CONSIDERATIONS

Today the choices of food for your Cairn Terrier are many and varied. There are simply dozens of brands of food in all sorts of flavours and textures, ranging from puppy diets to those for seniors. There are even hypoallergenic and low-calorie diets available. Because your Cairn Terrier's food has a bearing on coat, health and temperament, it is essential that the most suitable diet is selected for a Cairn Terrier of his age. It is fair to say, however, that even dedicated owners can be somewhat perplexed by the enormous range of foods available. Only understanding what is best for your dog will help you reach a valued decision.

Dog foods are produced in three basic types: dried, semi-moist and tinned. Dried foods are useful for the cost-conscious for overall they tend to be less expensive than semi-moist or tinned. These contain the least fat and the most preservatives. In general tinned foods are made up of 60–70 percent water, whilst semi-moist ones often contain so much sugar that they are perhaps the least preferred by owners, even though their dogs seem to like them.

When selecting your dog's diet, three stages of development must be considered: the puppy stage, adult stage and the senior or veteran stage.

PUPPY STAGE

Puppies instinctively want to suck milk from their mother's teats and

> ## Did You Know?
>
> You must store your dried dog food carefully. Open packages of dog food quickly lose their vitamin value, usually within 90 days of being opened. Mould spores and vermin could also contaminate the food.

> ## Did You Know?
>
> A good test for proper diet is the colour, odour, and firmness of your dog's stool. A healthy dog usually produces three semi-hard stools per day. The stools should have no unpleasant odour. They should be the same colour from excretion to excretion.

Food Preference

Selecting the best dried dog food is difficult. There is no majority consensus amongst veterinary scientists as to the value of nutrient analyses (protein, fat, fibre, moisture, ash, cholesterol, minerals, etc.). All agree that feeding trials are what matters, but you also have to consider the individual dog. Its weight, age, activity and what pleases its taste, all must be considered. It is probably best to take the advice of your veterinary surgeon. Every dog's dietary requirements vary, even during the lifetime of a particular dog.

If your dog is fed a good dried food, it does not require supplements of meat or vegetables. Dogs do appreciate a little variety in their diets so you may choose to stay with the same brand, but vary the flavour. Alternatively you may wish to add a little flavoured stock to give a difference to the taste.

a normal puppy will exhibit this behaviour from just a few moments following birth. If puppies do not attempt to suckle within the first half-hour or so, they should be encouraged to do so by placing them on the nipples, having selected ones with plenty of milk. This early milk supply is important in providing colostrum to protect the puppies during the first eight to ten weeks of their lives. Although a mother's milk is much better than any milk formula, despite there being some excellent ones available, if the puppies do not feed you will have to feed them yourself. For those with less experience, advice from a veterinary surgeon is important so that you feed not only the right quantity of milk but that of correct quality, fed at suitably frequent intervals, usually every two hours during the first few days of life.

Puppies should be allowed to nurse from their mothers for about the first six weeks, although from the third or fourth week you will have begun to introduce small portions of suitable solid food.

offer advice in this regard and, although the frequency of meals will have been reduced over time, only when a young dog has reached the age of about 18 months should an adult diet be fed.

Puppy and junior diets should be well balanced for the needs of your dog, so that except in certain circumstances additional vitamins, minerals and proteins will not be required.

ADULT DIETS

A dog is considered an adult when it has stopped growing, so in general the diet of a Cairn Terrier can be changed to an adult one at about 10 to 12 months of

Cairn puppies should be allowed to nurse for the first six weeks of their lives. By the time your Cairn is ready to come home, he will be completely weaned.

Most breeders like to introduce alternate milk and meat meals initially, building up to weaning time.

By the time the puppies are seven or a maximum of eight weeks old, they should be fully weaned and fed solely on a proprietary puppy food. Selection of the most suitable, good-quality diet at this time is essential for a puppy's fastest growth rate is during the first year of life. Veterinary surgeons are usually able to age. Again you should rely upon your veterinary surgeon or dietary specialist to recommend an acceptable maintenance diet. Major dog food manufacturers specialise in this type of food, and it is just necessary for you to select the one best suited to your dog's needs. Active dogs may have different requirements than sedate dogs.

SENIOR DIETS

As dogs get older, their metabolism changes. The older dog usually exercises less, moves more slowly and sleeps more. This change in lifestyle and physiological performance requires a change in diet. Since

Grain-Based Diets

Many adult diets are based on grain. There is nothing wrong with this as long as it does not contain soy meal. Diets based on soy often cause flatulence (passing gas).

Grain-based diets are almost always the least expensive and a good grain diet is just as good as the most expensive diet containing animal protein.

There are many cases, however, when your dog might require a special diet. These special requirements should only be recommended by your veterinary surgeon.

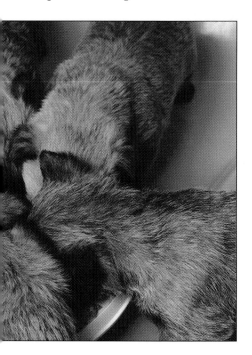

these changes take place slowly, they might not be recognisable. What is easily recognisable is weight gain. By continuing to feed your dog an adult-maintenance diet when it is slowing down metabolically, your dog will gain weight. Obesity in an older dog compounds the health problems that already accompany old age.

As dogs get older, few of their organs function up to par. The kidneys slow down and the intestines become less efficient. These age-related factors are best handled with a change in diet and a change in feeding schedule to give smaller portions that are more easily digested.

Competition around the feeding pan excites the appetites of young pups. Once the pup is brought into your home, he may 'wolf' his food voraciously. In time, he'll eat at a more leisurely pace.

There is no single best diet for every older dog. Whilst many dogs do well on light or senior diets, other dogs do better on puppy diets or other special premium diets such as lamb and rice. Be sensitive to your senior Cairn Terrier's diet and this will help control other problems that may arise with your old friend.

WATER

Just as your dog needs proper nutrition from his food, water is an essential 'nutrient' as well. Water keeps the dog's body properly hydrated and promotes normal function of the body's systems. During housebreaking it is necessary to keep an eye on how much water your Cairn Terrier is drinking, but once he is reliably trained he should have access to clean fresh water at all times. Make sure that the dog's water bowl is clean, and change the water often, making sure that water is always available for your dog, especially if you feed dried food.

Water must always be available for adults, unless there are medical reasons to withhold the water. During the housebreaking process, a pup's water intake must be monitored.

EXERCISE

Although a Cairn Terrier is small, all dogs require some form of exercise, regardless of breed. A sedentary lifestyle is as harmful to a dog as it is to a person. The Cairn Terrier is a fairly active breed that enjoys exercise, but you don't have to be an Olympic athlete! Regular walks, play sessions in the garden, or letting the dog run free in the garden under your supervision are sufficient forms of exercise for the Cairn Terrier. For those who are more ambitious, you will find that your Cairn Terrier also enjoys long walks, an occasional hike or even a swim! Bear in mind that an overweight dog should never be suddenly over-exercised; instead he should be allowed to increase exercise slowly. Not only is exercise essential to keep the dog's body fit, it is essential to his mental well being. A bored dog will find something to do, which often manifests itself in some type of destructive behaviour. In this sense, it is essential for the owner's mental well being as well!

GROOMING

Whether you have chosen the Cairn Terrier as a show dog or simply as a chum around your home, he will require a certain amount of grooming to look presentable and tidy. Although the Cairn's coat is not the most

What are you feeding your dog?

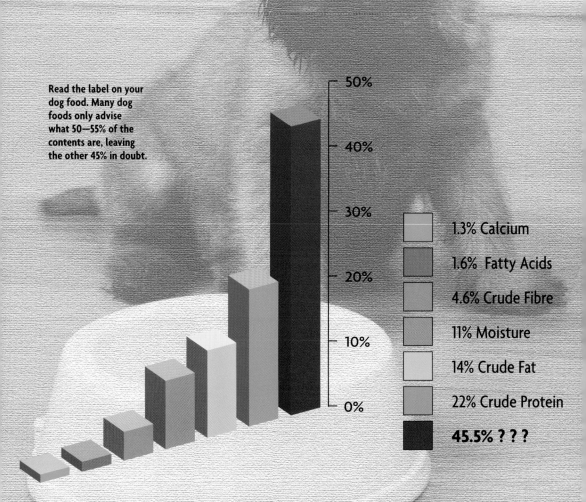

Read the label on your dog food. Many dog foods only advise what 50—55% of the contents are, leaving the other 45% in doubt.

50%

40%

30%

20%

10%

0%

1.3% Calcium

1.6% Fatty Acids

4.6% Crude Fibre

11% Moisture

14% Crude Fat

22% Crude Protein

45.5% ? ? ?

Your local pet shop has a wide supply of dog brushes from which you may select the ones that suit your needs.

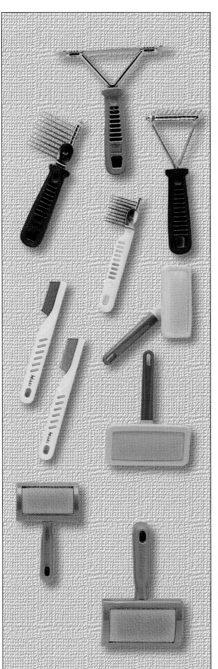

PHOTO COURTESY OF MIKKI PET PRODUCTS.

difficult coat in the Terrier Group to maintain, it will present demands on the owner. Remember, you cannot take a Cairn to a groomer and tell him to shave him down as you can a Poodle. This is a much different coat.

The Cairn is a double-coated dog. There is a dense, thick undercoat that protects the dog in all kinds of weather and there is a harsh outercoat. Coat care for the pet Cairn can be much less time-consuming and easier than the coat care for a show dog. The vast majority of Cairn fanciers has a dog for a pet and they should not expect to maintain a show coat.

If you are planning to show your Cairn Terrier, you are well advised to discuss the grooming and conditioning with the breeder from whom you acquired your

Grooming Equipment

Holland Buckley wrote in 1913: 'Most people wash their dogs regularly. Unless preparing a puppy for a special purpose, do not bathe him at all, at least not artificially, but get him used to swimming in a pond or the river, never forgetting to give him a good gallop and a rub down afterwards. A few minutes spent each day with a comb and a dandy brush will keep the coat in tip-top condition, and the skin supple and healthy.'

puppy. Most reputable breeders groom and show their own dogs. Visit the breeder with your puppy for grooming lessons to learn how to get your dog ready for the show ring. Grooming for the show is an art, and an art that cannot be learned in a few months. The primary difference between the pet and show Cairn coat is that the show Cairn will have a dense undercoat and on top of it he will have a tidy, harsh coat. With the proper coat, the dog presents a smartness in the ring that can be hard to beat. This coat can only be acquired by stripping the body coat, twice a year, with a stripping knife or stripping by hand. This all takes skill, time and interest in order to do it well. Pet grooming is different from grooming for the show ring and you will not have the harsh, tidy coat of the show Cairn, but you will have a neat, clean and trimmed dog that will still look like a Cairn Terrier.

In order to groom your Cairn Terrier yourself, you will need certain tools:

1. A grooming table, something sturdy with a rubber mat covering the top. You will need a grooming arm, or a 'hanger.' (You can use a table in your laundry room with an eye hook in the ceiling for holding the leash.) Your dog will now be comfortable even if confined and you will be able to work on the dog. Grooming is a very difficult

Getting ready for show presentation. A sturdy grooming table, adjustable to suit your height, is necessary to allow you to groom your Cairn comfortably.

and frustrating job if you try to groom without a table and a grooming arm.

2. A metal comb, a slicker brush, a good sharp pair of scissors and a toenail trimmer.

To start, set your dog on the table and put the leash around his neck. Have your leash up behind the ears and have the leash taut when you fasten it to your eye hook. Do not walk away and leave your dog unattended as he can jump off the table and be left dangling from the leash with his

69

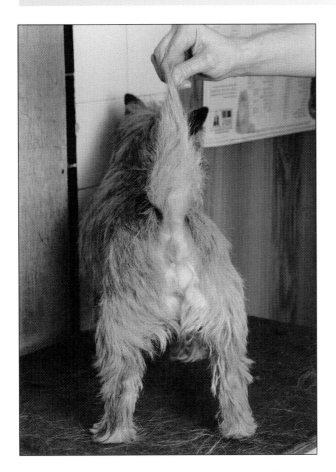

cleanliness, you may want to take your scissors and trim the area around the penis. With the girls, trim some of the hair around the vulva.

Now that your dog is brushed out, comb through the coat with your metal comb. By now you have removed a fair amount of dead hair and your dog will already be looking better. You may find some small matts and these can be worked out with your fingers or your comb. If you brush your dog out every week or so, you will not have too much of a problem with the matts.

When you find that the coat is separating, you should be prepared to do some hand-stripping, and this is pulling out the dead, long coat, in the direction in which it lies. It is best to have a stripping knife for this process and it is by far better if your breeder or someone else can show you how this is to be done. Of course, you can clip your dog down, leaving a trimmed head, and within eight to ten weeks, your dog will have a soft, but nice coat.

If this is your first experience, you may be a bit clumsy, but the hair will grow back in a short time. The finished product may not be quite what you had expected, but expertise will come with experience and you will soon be very proud of your efforts. Put your dog in the laundry tub

The Cairn's tail looks unkempt before the loose hairs are plucked. feet scrambling around in the air.

Take your slicker brush and brush out the entire coat. Brush the whiskers toward the nose, the body hair toward the tail, the tail up toward the tip of the tail. Brush the leg furnishings up toward the body and brush the chest hair down toward the table. Hold the dog up by the front legs and gently brush the stomach hair, first toward the head and then back toward the rear. For

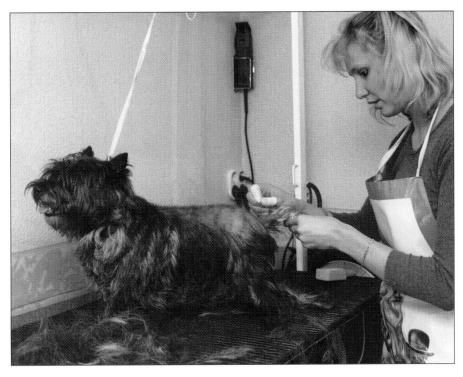

The Cairn is being trimmed and plucked. Notice the rubber fingertips on the groomer. These facilitate plucking.

when you are finished and give him a good bath and rinsing. After towelling him down, return him to the grooming table and trim the toenails on all four legs. At this point you can dry your dog with a blaster and brush him out again. Or, you can let him dry naturally and then brush him out. If you have grooming problems, you can take your dog to the professional groomer the first time or two for his grooming. (Of course, you can eliminate all of the grooming for yourself, except for the weekly brushing, if you take your dog to the groomer every three months!) Just remember, many pet owners

Your Cairn may never truly appreciate the grooming process, but he will learn to accept it. This type of training starts at an early age. For such small terriers, they certainly cast an abundant coat.

71

(Facing page) The Cairn being bathed. First the dog is wet down thoroughly. Then dog shampoo is applied and rubbed in using the same technique you would use when shampooing your own hair. Finally, using warm water, the shampoo is thoroughly washed out of the coat. Some groomers repeat this process in order to be sure the coat is clean.

Grooming Tip

The use of human soap products like shampoo, bubble bath and hand soap can be damaging to a dog's coat and skin. Human products are too strong and remove the protective oils coating the dog's hair and skin (making him water-resistant). Use only shampoo made especially for dogs and you may like to use a medicated shampoo, which will always help to keep external parasites at bay.

could end up a wet, soapy, messy ordeal for both of you!

Brush your Cairn Terrier thoroughly before wetting his coat. This will get rid of most matts and tangles, which are harder to remove when the coat is wet. Make that your dog has a good non-slip surface to stand on. Begin by wetting the dog's coat. A shower or hose attachment is necessary for thoroughly wetting and rinsing the coat. Check the water temperature to make sure that it is neither too hot nor too cold.

Next, apply shampoo to the dog's coat and work it into a good

can do a much better job trimming their dogs than some professional groomers.

In general, your pet should be brushed weekly and bathed as needed. Trim the toenails every month or so and plan to clip the dog every three months. Follow this plan and your dog will be clean, he will have a new 'dress' every three months, and he will look like a Cairn Terrier!

BATHING

Dogs do not need to be bathed as often as humans, but regular bathing is essential for healthy skin and a healthy, shiny coat. Again, like most anything, if you accustom your pup to being bathed as a puppy, it will be second nature by the time he grows up. You want your dog to be at ease in the bath or else it

Grooming Tip

Once you are sure that the dog is thoroughly rinsed, squeeze the excess water out of the coat with your hand and dry him with a heavy towel. You may choose to use a blaster on his coat or just let it dry naturally. In cold weather, never allow your dog outside with a wet coat.

There are 'dry bath' products on the market, which are sprays and powders intended for spot cleaning, that can be used between regular baths, if necessary. They are not substitutes for regular baths, but they are easy to use for touch-ups as they do not require rinsing.

lather. You should purchase a shampoo that is made for dogs. Do not use a product made for human hair. Wash the head last; you do not want shampoo to drip into the dog's eyes whilst you are washing the rest of his body. Work the shampoo all the way down to the skin. You can use this opportunity to check the skin for any bumps, bites or other abnormalities. Do not neglect any area of the body—get all of the hard-to-reach places.

Once the dog has been thoroughly shampooed, he requires an equally thorough rinsing. Shampoo left in the coat can be irritating to the skin. Protect his eyes from the shampoo by shielding them with your hand and directing the flow of water in the opposite direction. You should also avoid getting water in the ear canal. Be prepared for your dog to shake out his coat—you might want to stand back, but make sure you have a hold on the dog to keep him from running through the house.

EAR CLEANING

The ears should be kept clean and any excess hair inside the ear should be carefully plucked out. Ears can be cleaned with cotton wipes made especially for dogs and specifically for this purpose. Be on the lookout for any signs of infection or ear mite infestation. If your Cairn Terrier has been shaking his head or scratching at

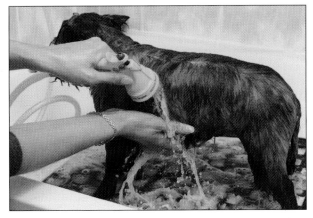

Before you start cutting, make sure you can identify the 'quick' in each nail. The quick is a blood vessel that runs through the centre of each nail and grows rather close to the end. It will bleed if accidentally cut, which will be quite painful for the dog as it contains nerve endings. Keep some type of clotting agent on hand, such as a styptic pencil or styptic powder (the type used for shaving). This will stop the bleeding quickly when applied to the end of the cut nail. Do not panic if this happens, just stop the bleeding and talk soothingly to your dog. Once he has calmed down, move on to the next nail. It is better to clip a little at a time,

A blaster should be used to dry the Cairn's coat thoroughly. Be careful that the air is not too hot for the dog's delicate skin.

his ears frequently, this usually indicates a problem. If his ears have an unusual odour, this is a sure sign of mite infestation or infection, and a signal to have his ears checked by the veterinary surgeon.

NAIL CLIPPING
Your Cairn Terrier should be accustomed to having his nails trimmed at an early age, since it will be part of your maintenance routine throughout his life. Not only does it look nicer, but long nails can be sharp if they scratch someone unintention-ally. Also, a long nail has a better chance of ripping and bleeding, or causing the feet to spread. A good rule of thumb is that if you can hear your dog's nails clicking on the floor when he walks, his nails are too long.

The ears should be cleaned with cotton wipes made especially for dogs. Be alert to ear mites or any debris that might be visible whilst you are cleaning the ear.

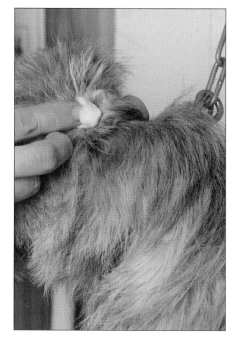

Nail Clipping

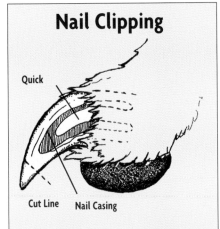

Quick

Cut Line   Nail Casing

DARK-COLOURED NAIL

With black or dark nails, it's best to clip only a small bit of the nail at a time or to use a file where the quick is not visible.

LIGHT-COLOURED NAIL

In light-coloured nails, clipping is much simpler because you can see the vein (or quick) that grows inside the casing.

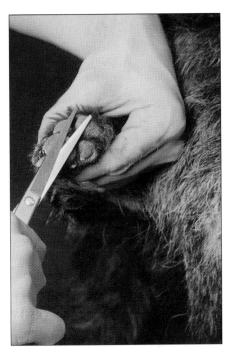

The hair on the bottom of the foot must be trimmed carefully.

Pet shops have special clippers for your dog's nails. Be sure the clippers are sharp.

particularly with black-nailed dogs.

Hold your pup steady as you begin trimming his nails; you do not want him to make any sudden movements or run away. Talk to him soothingly and stroke him as you clip. Holding his foot in your hand, simply take off the end of each nail in one quick clip. You can purchase nail clippers that are specially made for dogs; you can probably find them wherever you buy pet or grooming supplies.

TRAVELLING WITH YOUR DOG
CAR TRAVEL

You should accustom your Cairn Terrier to riding in a car at an early age. You may or may not take him in the car often, but at the very least he will need to go to the vet and you do not want these trips to be traumatic for the dog or a big hassle for you. The safest way for a dog to ride in the car is in his crate. If he uses a crate in the house, you can use the same crate for travel.

Put the pup in the crate and see how he reacts. If he seems uneasy, you can have a passenger hold him on his lap whilst you drive. Another option is a specially made safety harness for dogs, which straps the dog in

Your Cairn Terrier should never be allowed complete freedom in your car whilst you are driving.

much like a seat belt. Do not let the dog roam loose in the vehicle—this is very dangerous! If you should stop short, your dog can be thrown and injured. If the dog starts climbing on you and pestering you whilst you are driving, you will not be able to concentrate on the road. It is an

unsafe situation for everyone—human and canine.

For long trips, be prepared to stop to let the dog relieve himself. Bring along whatever you need to clean up after him. You should take along some paper kitchen

Travel Tip

When travelling, never let your dog off-lead in a strange area. Your dog could run away out of fear or decide to chase a passing chipmunk or cat or simply want to stretch his legs without restriction—you might never see your canine friend again.

The Cairn is a small enough dog to be able to comfortably be restrained in a crate in your car.

towels and perhaps some old towelling for use should he have an accident in the car or suffer from travel sickness.

AIR TRAVEL

Whilst it is possible to take a dog on a flight within Britain, this is fairly unusual and advance permission is always required. The dog will be required to travel in a fibreglass crate and you should always check in advance with the airline regarding specific requirements. To help the dog be at ease, put one of his favourite toys in the crate with him. Do not feed the dog for at least six hours before the trip to minimise his need to relieve himself. However, certain regulations specify that water must always be made available to the dog in the crate.

Make sure your dog is properly identified and that your contact information appears on his ID tags and on his crate. Animals travel in a different area

Travel Tip

If you are going on a long motor trip with your dog, be sure the hotels are dog friendly. Many hotels do not accept dogs. Also take along some ice that can be thawed and offered to your dog if he becomes overheated. Most dogs like to lick ice.

Travel Tip

For international travel you will have to make arrangements well in advance (perhaps months), as countries' regulations pertaining to bringing in animals differ. There may be special health certificates and/or vaccinations that your dog will need before taking the trip, sometimes this has to be done within a certain time frame. In rabies-free countries, you will need to bring proof of the dog's rabies vaccination and there may be a quarantine period upon arrival.

of the plane than human passengers so every rule must be strictly adhered to so as to prevent the risk of getting separated from your dog.

BOARDING

So you want to take a family holiday—and you want to include all members of the family. You would probably make arrangements for accommodations ahead of time anyway, but this is especially important when travelling with a dog. You do not want to make an overnight stop at the only place around for miles and find out that they do not allow dogs. Also, you do not want to reserve a place for your family without confirming that you are

travelling with a dog because if it is against their policy you may not have a place to stay.

Alternatively, if you are travelling and choose not to bring your Cairn Terrier, you will have to make arrangements for him whilst you are away. Some options are to take him to a neighbour's house to stay whilst you are gone, to have a trusted neighbour call round often or stay at your house, or bring your dog to a reputable boarding kennel. If you choose to board him at a kennel, you should visit in advance to see the facilities provided, how clean they are and where the dogs are kept. Talk to some of the employees and see how they treat the dogs—do they spend time with the dogs, play with them, exercise them, etc.? Also find out the kennel's policy on vaccinations and what they

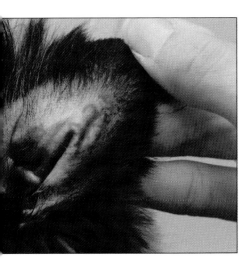

require. This is for all of the dogs' safety, since when dogs are kept together, there is a greater risk of diseases being passed from dog to dog.

IDENTIFICATION
Your Cairn Terrier is your valued companion and friend. That is why you always keep a close eye on him and you have made sure that he cannot escape from the garden or wriggle out of his collar and run away from you. However, accidents can happen and there may come a time when your dog unexpectedly gets separated from you. If this unfortunate event should occur, the first thing on your mind will be finding him. Proper identification, including an ID tag, a tattoo and possibly a microchip, will increase the chances of his being returned to you safely and quickly.

Many valuable Cairns are tattooed underneath their ears (or inside their thighs) so they can be identified if lost or stolen.

Living with an untrained dog is a lot like owning a piano that you do not know how to play—it is a nice object to look at but it does not do much more than that to bring you pleasure. Now try taking piano lessons and suddenly the piano comes alive and brings forth magical sounds and rhythms that set your heart singing and your body swaying.

The same is true with your Cairn Terrier. Any dog is a big responsibility and if not trained sensibly may develop unacceptable behaviour that annoys you or could even cause family friction.

To train your Cairn Terrier, you may like to enrol in an

Did You Know?

If you start with a normal, healthy dog and give him time, patience and some carefully executed lessons, you will reap the rewards of that training for the life of the dog. And what a life it will be! The two of you will find immeasurable pleasure in the companionship you have built together with love, respect and understanding.

obedience class. Teach him good manners as you learn how and why he behaves the way he does. Find out how to communicate with your dog and how to recognise and understand his communications with you. Suddenly the dog takes on a new role in your life—he is clever, interesting, well behaved and fun to be with. He demonstrates his bond of devotion to you daily. In other words, your Cairn Terrier does wonders for your ego because he constantly reminds you that you are not only his leader, you are his hero!

Those involved with teaching dog obedience and

Obedience School

Taking your dog to an obedience school may be the best investment in time and money you can ever make. You will enjoy the benefits for the lifetime of your dog and you will have the opportunity to meet people with your similar expectations for companion dogs.

Did You Know?

To a dog's way of thinking, your hands are like his mouth in terms of a defence mechanism. If you squeeze him too tightly, he might just bite you because that would be his normal response. This is not aggressive biting and, although all biting should be discouraged, you need the discipline in learning how to handle your dog.

An eight-week-old Cairn puppy with a collar and lead attached for the first time. Cairns usually refuse to move or be pulled. The basis of HEEL training starts straight away!

counselling owners about their dogs' behaviour have discovered some interesting facts about dog ownership. For example, training dogs when they are puppies results in the highest rate of success in developing well-mannered and well-adjusted adult dogs. Training an older dog, from six months to six years of age, can produce almost equal results providing that the owner accepts the dog's slower rate of learning capability and is willing to work patiently to help the dog succeed at developing to his fullest potential. Unfortunately, many owners of untrained adult dogs lack the patience factor, so they do not persist until their dogs are successful at learning particular behaviours.

Training a puppy aged 10 to 16 weeks (20 weeks at the most)

is like working with a dry sponge in a pool of water. The pup soaks up whatever you show him and constantly looks

Training Tip

Training a dog is a life experience. Many parents admit that much of what they know about raising children they learned from caring for their dogs. Dogs respond to love, fairness and guidance, just as children do. Become a good dog owner and you may become an even better parent.

81

for more things to do and learn. At this early age, his body is not yet producing hormones, and therein lies the reason for such a high rate of success. Without hormones, he is focused on his owners and not particularly interested in investigating other places, dogs, people, etc. You are his leader: his provider of food, water, shelter and security. He latches onto you and wants to stay close. He will usually follow you from room to room, will not let you out of his sight when you are outdoors with him, and respond in like manner to the people and animals you encounter. If you greet a friend warmly, he will be happy to greet the person as well. If, however, you are hesitant, even anxious, about the approach of a stranger, he will respond accordingly.

Once the puppy begins to

Think Before You Bark!

Dogs are sensitive to their master's moods and emotions. Use your voice wisely when communicating with your dog. Never raise your voice at your dog unless you are angry and trying to correct him. 'Barking' at your dog can become as meaningless as 'dogspeak' is to you. Think before you bark!

Did You Know?

Dogs will do anything for your attention. If you reward the dog when he is calm and resting, you will develop a well-mannered dog. If, on the other hand, you greet your dog excitedly and encourage him to wrestle and roughhouse with you, the dog will greet you the same way and you will have a hyper dog on your hands.

produce hormones, his natural curiosity emerges and he begins to investigate the world around him. It is at this time when you may notice that the untrained dog begins to wander away from you and even ignore your commands to stay close. When this behaviour becomes a problem, the owner has two choices: get rid of the dog or train him. It is strongly urged that you choose the latter option.

There are usually classes within a reasonable distance from the owner's home, but you also do a lot to train your dog yourself. Sometimes there are classes available but the tuition is too costly. Whatever the circumstances, the solution to the problem of lack of lesson availability lies within the pages of this book.

This chapter is devoted to

helping you train your Cairn Terrier at home. If the recommended procedures are followed faithfully, you may expect positive results that will prove rewarding to both you and your dog.

Whether your new charge is a puppy or a mature adult, the methods of teaching and the techniques we use in training basic behaviours are the same. After all, no dog, whether puppy or adult, likes harsh or inhumane methods. All creatures, however, respond favourably to gentle motivational methods and sincere praise and encouragement. Now let us get started.

HOUSEBREAKING

You can train a puppy to relieve itself wherever you choose, but this must be somewhere suitable.

You should bear in mind from the outset that when your puppy is old enough to go out in public places, any canine deposits must be removed at once. You will always have to carry with you a

You must train your Cairn to relieve himself when and where YOU want. All deposits should be cleaned up even if they are left in your own garden.

small plastic bag or 'poop-scoop.'

Outdoor training includes such surfaces as grass, soil and cement. Indoor training usually means training your dog to newspaper.

When deciding on the surface and location that you will want your Cairn Terrier to use, be sure it is going to be permanent. Training your dog to grass and then changing your mind two months later is extremely difficult for both dog and owner.

Next, choose the command you will use each and every time you want your puppy to void. 'Hurry up' and 'Toilet' are examples of commands commonly used by dog owners.

Did You Know?

Never line your pup's sleeping area with newspaper. Puppy litters are usually raised on newspaper and, once in your home, the puppy will immediately associate newspaper with voiding. Never put newspaper on any floor while housetraining, as this will only confuse the puppy. If you are paper-training him, use paper in his designated relief area ONLY. Finally, restrict water intake after evening meals. Offer a few licks at a time—never let a young puppy gulp water after meals.

Did You Know?

Dogs are the most honourable animals in existence. They consider another species (humans) as their own. They interface with you. You are their leader. Puppies perceive children to be on their level; their actions around small children are different than their behaviour around their adult masters.

Get in the habit of giving the puppy your chosen relief command before you take him out. That way, when he becomes an adult, you will be able to determine if he wants to go out when you ask him. A confirmation will be signs of interest, wagging his tail, watching you intently, going to the door, etc.

PUPPY'S NEEDS

Puppy needs to relieve himself after play periods, after each meal, after he has been sleeping and any time he indicates that he is looking for a place to urinate or defecate.

The urinary and intestinal tract muscles of very young puppies are not fully developed. Therefore, like human babies, puppies need to relieve themselves frequently.

Take your puppy out often— every hour for an eight-week-old,

Canine Development Schedule

It is important to understand how and at what age a puppy develops into adulthood.
If you are a puppy owner, consult the following Canine Development Schedule to
determine the stage of development your puppy is currently experiencing.
This knowledge will help you as you work with the puppy in the weeks and months ahead.

Period	Age	Characteristics
FIRST TO THIRD	BIRTH TO SEVEN WEEKS	Puppy needs food, sleep and warmth, and responds to simple and gentle touching. Needs mother for security and disciplining. Needs littermates for learning and interacting with other dogs. Pup learns to function within a pack and learns pack order of dominance. Begin socialising with adults and children for short periods. Begins to become aware of its environment.
FOURTH	EIGHT TO TWELVE WEEKS	Brain is fully developed. Needs socialising with outside world. Remove from mother and littermates. Needs to change from canine pack to human pack. Human dominance necessary. Fear period occurs between 8 and 16 weeks. Avoid fright and pain.
FIFTH	THIRTEEN TO SIXTEEN WEEKS	Training and formal obedience should begin. Less association with other dogs, more with people, places, situations. Period will pass easily if you remember this is pup's change-to-adolescence time. Be firm and fair. Flight instinct prominent. Permissiveness and over-disciplining can do permanent damage. Praise for good behaviour.
JUVENILE	FOUR TO EIGHT MONTHS	Another fear period about 7 to 8 months of age. It passes quickly, but be cautious of fright and pain. Sexual maturity reached. Dominant traits established. Dog should understand sit, down, come and stay by now.

NOTE: THESE ARE APPROXIMATE TIME FRAMES. ALLOW FOR INDIVIDUAL DIFFERENCES IN PUPPIES.

Training Tip

Your dog is actually training you at the same time you are training him. Dogs do things to get attention. They usually repeat whatever succeeds in getting your attention.

for example, and always immediately after sleeping and eating. The older the puppy, the less often he will need to relieve himself. Finally, as a mature healthy adult, he will require only three to five relief trips per day.

HOUSING

Since the type of housing and control you provide for your puppy has a direct relationship on the success of housetraining, we consider the various aspects of both before we begin training.

Housebreaking Tip

Do not carry your dog to his toilet area. Lead him there on a leash or, better yet, encourage him to follow you to the spot. If you start carrying him to his spot, you might end up doing this routine forever and your dog will have the satisfaction of having trained YOU.

Bringing a new puppy home and turning him loose in your house can be compared to turning a child loose in a sports arena and telling the child that the place is all his! The sheer enormity of the place would be too much for him to handle.

Instead, offer the puppy clearly defined areas where he can play, sleep, eat and live. A room of the house where the family gathers is the most obvious choice. Puppies are

Training Tip

Stand up straight and authoritatively when giving your dog commands. Do not issue commands when lying on the floor or lying on your back on the sofa. If you are on your hands and knees when you give a command, your dog will think you are positioning yourself to play.

social animals and need to feel a part of the pack right from the start. Hearing your voice, watching you whilst you are doing things and smelling you nearby are all positive reinforcers that he is now a member of your pack. Usually a family room, the kitchen or a nearby adjoining breakfast area is ideal for providing safety and security for both puppy and owner.

Practice Makes Perfect!

• Have training lessons with your dog every day in several short segments—three to five times a day for a few minutes at a time is ideal.

• Do not have long practice sessions. The dog will become easily bored.

• Never practise when you are tired, ill, worried or in an otherwise negative mood. This will transmit to the dog and may have an adverse effect on its performance.

Think fun, short and above all POSITIVE! End each session on a high note, rather than a failed exercise, and make sure to give a lot of praise. Enjoy the training and help your dog enjoy it, too.

Wire crates are usually available at pet shops in a KD (knocked-down) version. Be sure there is a suitable location for a stable water supply.

animals and will not remain close to their relief areas unless forced to do so. In those cases, they then become dirty dogs and usually remain that way for life.

The designated area should be lined with clean bedding and a toy. Water must always be available, in a non-spill container.

CONTROL

By control, we mean helping the puppy to create a lifestyle pattern that will be compatible to that of his human pack (YOU!).

Within that room there should be a smaller area which the puppy can call his own. An alcove, a wire or fibreglass dog crate or a fenced (not boarded!) corner from which he can view the activities of his new family will be fine. The size of the area or crate is the key factor here. The area must be large enough for the puppy to lie down and stretch out as well as stand up without rubbing his head on the top, yet small enough so that he cannot relieve himself at one end and sleep at the other without coming into contact with his droppings until fully trained to relieve himself outside.

Dogs are, by nature, clean

The Golden Rule

The golden rule of dog training is simple. For each 'question' (command), there is only one correct answer (reaction). One command = one reaction. Keep practising the command until the dog reacts correctly without hesitating. Be repetitive but not monotonous. Dogs get bored just as people do!

At 11 weeks of age, this Cairn required 10 relief trips per day! Some dogs drink and eat more than others and therefore require more relief trips.

How Many Times A Day?

AGE	RELIEF TRIPS
To 14 weeks	10
14–22 weeks	8
22–32 weeks	6
Adulthood	4
(dog stops growing)	

These are estimates, of course, but they are a guide to the MINIMUM opportunities a dog should have each day to relieve itself.

Just as we guide little children to learn our way of life, we must show the puppy when it is time to play, eat, sleep, exercise and even entertain himself.

Your puppy should always sleep in his crate. He should also learn that, during times of household confusion and excessive human activity such as at breakfast when family members are preparing for the day, he can play by himself in relative safety and comfort in his designated area. Each time you leave the puppy alone, he should understand exactly where he is to stay. Puppies are chewers. They cannot tell the difference between lamp cords, television wires, shoes, table legs, etc. Chewing into a television wire, for example, can be fatal to the puppy whilst a shorted wire can start a fire in the house.

If the puppy chews on the arm of the chair when he is alone, you will probably discipline him angrily when you get home. Thus, he makes the association that your coming home means he is going to be punished. (He will not remember chewing up the chair and is incapable of making the association of the discipline with his naughty deed.)

Other times of excitement, such as family parties, etc., can be fun for the puppy providing he can view the activities from the security of his designated area. He is not underfoot and he is not being fed all sorts of titbits that will probably cause him stomach distress, yet he still feels a part of the fun.

Always clean up after your dog, whether you're in a public place or your own garden.

SCHEDULE

A puppy should be taken to his relief area each time he is released from his designated area, after meals, after a play session, when he first awakens in the morning (at age eight weeks, this can mean 5 a.m.!). The puppy will indicate that he's ready 'to go' by circling or sniffing busily—do not misinterpret these signs. For a puppy less than ten weeks of age, a routine of taking him out every hour is necessary. As the puppy grows, he will be able to wait for longer periods of time.

THE SUCCESS METHOD
6 Steps to Successful Crate Training

1 Tell the puppy 'Crate time!' and place him in the crate with a small treat (a piece of cheese or half of a biscuit). Let him stay in the crate for five minutes while you are in the same room. Then release him and praise lavishly. Never release him when he is fussing. Wait until he is quiet before you let him out.

2 Repeat Step 1 several times a day.

3 The next day, place the puppy in the crate as before. Let him stay there for ten minutes. Do this several times.

4 Continue building time in five-minute increments until the puppy stays in his crate for 30 minutes with you in the room. Always take him to his relief area after prolonged periods in his crate.

5 Now go back to Step 1 and let the puppy stay in his crate for five minutes, this time while you are out of the room.

6 Once again, build crate time in five-minute increments with you out of the room. When the puppy will stay willingly in his crate (he may even fall asleep!) for 30 minutes with you out of the room, he will be ready to stay in it for several hours at a time.

Keep trips to his relief area short. Stay no more than five or six minutes and then return to the house. If he goes during that time, praise him lavishly and take him indoors immediately. If he does not, but he has an accident when you go back indoors, pick him up immediately, say 'No! No!' and return to his relief area. Wait a few minutes, then return to the house again. Never hit a puppy or rub his face in urine or excrement when he has an accident!

Once indoors, put the puppy in his crate until you have had time to clean up his accident. Then release him to the family area and watch him more closely than before. Chances are, his accident was a result of your not

Did You Know?

If you want to be successful in training your dog, you have four rules to obey yourself:
1. Develop an understanding of how a dog thinks.
2. Do not blame the dog for lack of communication.
3. Define your dog's person-ality and act accordingly.
4. Have patience and be consistent.

picking up his signal or waiting too long before offering him the opportunity to relieve himself. Never hold a grudge against the puppy for accidents.

Let the puppy learn that going outdoors means it is time to relieve himself, not play. Once trained, he will be able to play indoors and out and still differen-tiate between the times for play versus the times for relief.

Help him develop regular hours for naps, being alone, playing by himself and just resting, all in his crate. Encourage him to entertain himself whilst you are busy with your activities. Let him learn that having you near is comforting, but it is not your main purpose in life to provide him with undivided attention.

Each time you put a puppy in his own area, use the same command, whatever suits best.

Did You Know?

The puppy should also have regular play and exercise sessions when he is with you or a family member. Exercise for a very young puppy can consist of a short walk around the house or garden. Playing can include fetching games with a large ball or a special raggy. (All puppies teethe and need soft things upon which to chew.) Remember to restrict play periods to indoors within his living area (the family room for example) until he is completely housetrained.

Soon, he will run to his crate or special area when he hears you say those words.

Crate training provides safety for you, the puppy and the home. It also provides the puppy with a feeling of security, and that helps the puppy achieve self-confidence and clean habits.

Remember that one of the primary ingredients in housetraining your puppy is control. Regardless of your lifestyle, there will always be occasions when you will need to have a place where your dog can stay and be happy and safe. Training is the answer for now and in the future.

Eight weeks old and ready for a new life. Help him to develop a schedule of naps, relief trips and play. He depends on you to help him to adjust to your life. Don't allow HIM to train YOU.

In conclusion, a few key elements are really all you need for a successful house training

Training Tip

Never train your dog, puppy or adult, when you are angry or in a sour mood. Dogs are very sensitive to human feelings, especially anger, and if your dog senses that you are angry or upset, he will connect your anger with his training and learn to resent or fear his training sessions.

Did You Know?

Dogs do not understand our language. They can be trained to react to a certain sound, at a certain volume. If you say 'No, Oliver' in a very soft pleasant voice it will not have the same meaning as 'No, Oliver!!' when you shout it as loud as you can. You should never use the dog's name during a reprimand, just the command NO!! Since dogs don't understand words, comics use dogs trained with opposite meanings. Thus, when the comic commands his dog to SIT the dog will stand up; and vice versa.

method—consistency, frequency, praise, control and supervision. By following these procedures with a normal, healthy puppy, you and the puppy will soon be past the stage of 'accidents' and ready to move on to a full and rewarding life together.

Digging holes in the sand in search of something edible...like sand crabs. Cairns are both diggers and natural hunters.

ROLES OF DISCIPLINE, REWARD AND PUNISHMENT

Discipline, training one to act in accordance with rules, brings order to life. It is as simple as that. Without discipline, particularly in a group society, chaos reigns supreme and the group will eventually perish. Humans and canines are social animals and need some form of discipline in order to function effectively. They must procure food, protect their home base and their young and reproduce to keep the species going.

If there were no discipline in the lives of social animals, they would eventually die from starvation and/or predation by other stronger animals.

In the case of domestic canines, dogs need discipline in their lives in order to understand how their pack (you and other family members) functions and how they must act in order to survive.

A large humane society in a highly populated area recently surveyed dog owners regarding their satisfaction with their relationships with their dogs. People who had trained their dogs were 75% more satisfied with their pets than those who had never trained their dogs.

Dr Edward Thorndike, a psychologist, established *Thorndike's Theory of Learning*, which states that a behaviour that results in a pleasant event tends to be repeated. A behaviour that results in an unpleasant event tends not to be repeated. It is this theory on which training methods are based today. For example, if you manipulate a dog to perform a specific behaviour and reward him for doing it, he is likely to do it again because he enjoyed the end result.

Occasionally, punishment, a penalty inflicted for an offence, is

Did You Know?

Dogs are as different from each other as people are. What works for one dog may not work for another. Have an open mind. If one method of training is unsuccessful, try another.

necessary. The best type of punishment often comes from an outside source. For example, a child is told not to touch the stove because he may get burned. He disobeys and touches the stove. In doing so, he receives a

TRAINING EQUIPMENT
COLLAR AND LEAD
For a Cairn Terrier the collar and lead that you use for training must be one with which you are easily able to work, not too heavy for the dog and perfectly safe.

You can easily bribe your Cairn puppy using a tasty treat.

burn. From that time on, he respects the heat of the stove and avoids contact with it. Therefore, a behaviour that results in an unpleasant event tends not to be repeated.

A good example of a dog learning the hard way is the dog who chases the house cat. He is told many times to leave the cat alone, yet he persists in teasing the cat. Then, one day he begins chasing the cat but the cat turns and swipes a claw across the dog's face, leaving him with a painful gash on his nose. The final result is that the dog stops chasing the cat.

TREATS
Have a bag of treats on hand. Something nutritious and easy to swallow works best. Use a soft treat, a chunk of cheese or a piece of cooked chicken rather than a dry biscuit. By the time the dog has finished chewing a dry treat, he will forget why he is being rewarded in the first place! Using food rewards will not teach a dog to beg at the table—the only way to teach a dog to beg at the table is to give him food from the table. In training, rewarding the dog with a food treat will help him associate praise and the treats with learning new behaviours that obviously please his owner.

Watching a treat in your hand, the Cairn is fully alert, wondering what your next move will be. He intends to please you so he can earn the treat. This is the basis of training with treats.

your hand as you approach within a foot of the dog. Do not go directly to him, but stop about a foot short of him and hold out the treat as you ask, 'School?' He will see you approaching with a treat in your hand and most likely begin walking toward you. As you meet, give him the treat and praise again.

The third time, ask the question, have a treat in your hand and walk only a short distance toward the dog so that he must walk almost all the way to you. As he reaches you, give him the treat and praise again.

By this time, the dog will probably be getting the idea that if he pays attention to you, especially when you ask that question, it will pay off in treats

TRAINING BEGINS: ASK THE DOG A QUESTION

In order to teach your dog anything, you must first get his attention. After all, he cannot learn anything if he is looking away from you with his mind on something else.

To get his attention, ask him, 'School?' and immediately walk over to him and give him a treat as you tell him 'Good dog.' Wait a minute or two and repeat the routine, this time with a treat in

and fun activities for him. In other words, he learns that 'school' means doing fun things with you that result in treats and positive attention for him.

Remember that the dog does not understand your verbal language, he only recognises sounds. Your question translates to a series of sounds for him, and those sounds become the signal to go to you and pay attention; if he does, he will get to interact with you plus receive treats and praise.

THE BASIC COMMANDS
TEACHING SIT
Now that you have the dog's attention, attach his lead and hold it in your left hand and a food treat in your right. Place your food hand at the dog's nose and let him

Once the Cairn assumes a proper sit position, make him hold it before rewarding him.

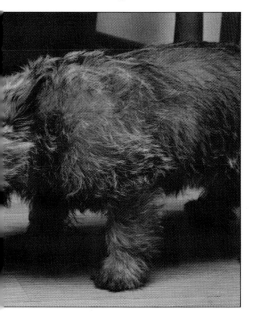

lick the treat but not take it from you. Say 'Sit' and slowly raise your food hand from in front of the dog's nose up over his head so that he is looking at the ceiling. As he bends his head upward, he will have to bend his knees to maintain his balance. As he bends his knees, he will assume a sit position. At that point, release the food treat and praise lavishly with comments such as 'Good dog! Good sit!', etc. Remember to always praise enthusiastically, because dogs relish verbal praise from their owners and feel so proud of themselves whenever

Puppies have a way of always being 'underfoot.' You don't want your Cairn chewing on your shoe laces, whether or not you are wearing the shoes!

95

they accomplish a behaviour.

You will not use food forever in getting the dog to obey your commands. Food is only used to teach new behaviours, and once the dog knows what you want when you give a specific command, you will wean him off of the food treats but still maintain the verbal praise. After all, you will always have your

The dog is taught the DOWN position from the SIT position. Teaching DOWN is not an easy exercise because dogs feel insecure in the down position.

voice with you, and there will be many times when you have no food rewards but expect the dog to obey.

TEACHING DOWN

Teaching the down exercise is easy when you understand how the dog perceives the down position, and it is very difficult when you do not. Dogs perceive the down position as a submissive one, therefore teaching the down exercise using a forceful method can sometimes make the dog develop such a fear of the down that he either runs away when you say 'Down' or he attempts to snap at the person who tries to force him down.

Have the dog sit close alongside your left leg, facing in the same direction as you are. Hold the lead in your left hand and a food treat in your right. Now place your left hand lightly on the top of the dog's shoulders where they meet above the spinal cord. Do not push down on the dog's shoulders; simply rest your left hand there so you can guide the dog to lie down close to your left leg rather than to swing away from your side when he drops.

Now place the food hand at the dog's nose, say 'Down' very softly (almost a whisper), and slowly lower the food hand to the dog's front feet. When the food hand reaches the floor, begin moving it forward along the floor

Did You Know?

A dog in jeopardy never lies down. He stays alert on his feet because instinct tells him that he may have to run away or fight for his survival. Therefore, if a dog feels threatened or anxious, he will not lie down. Consequently, it is important to have the dog calm and relaxed as he learns the down exercise.

in front of the dog. Keep talking softly to the dog, saying things like, 'Do you want this treat? You can do this, good dog.' Your reassuring tone of voice will help calm the dog as he tries to follow the food hand in order to get the treat.

When the dog's elbows touch the floor, release the food and praise softly. Try to get the dog to maintain that down position for several seconds before you let him sit up again. The goal here is to get the dog to settle down and not feel threatened in the down position.

TEACHING STAY

It is easy to teach the dog to stay in either a sit or a down position. Again, we use food and praise during the teaching process as we help the dog to understand exactly what it is that we are expecting him to do.

To teach the sit/stay, start with the dog sitting on your left side as before and hold the lead in your left hand. Have a food treat in your right hand and place your food hand at the dog's nose. Say 'Stay' and step out on your right foot to stand directly in front of the dog, toe to toe, as he licks and nibbles the treat. Be sure to keep his head facing upward to maintain the sit position. Count to five and then swing around to stand next to the dog again with him on your left. As soon as you

Teaching a dog to STAY in the sit or down position is not difficult. This exercise increases your Cairn's patience and obedience.

get back to the original position, release the food and praise lavishly.

To teach the down/stay, do the down as previously described. As soon as the dog lies down, say 'Stay' and step out on your right foot just as you did in the sit/stay.

A Cairn puppy is mouldable and attentive. This eight-week-old toddler has just had his coat plucked for the first time.

nose. He will watch the food hand and quickly learn that he is going to get that treat as soon as you return to his side.

When you can stand 1 metre away from your dog for 30 seconds, you can then begin building time and distance in both stays. Eventually, the dog can be expected to remain in the stay position for prolonged periods of time until you return to him or call him to you. Always praise lavishly when he stays.

TEACHING COME

If you make teaching 'come' a fun experience, you should never have a 'student' that does not love the game or that fails to come when called. The secret, it seems, is never to teach the word 'come.'

At times when an owner most wants his dog to come when called, the owner is likely to be upset or anxious and he allows

Count to five and then return to stand beside the dog with him on your left side. Release the treat and praise as always.

Within a week or ten days, you can begin to add a bit of distance between you and your dog when you leave him. When you do, use your left hand open with the palm facing the dog as a stay signal, much the same as the hand signal a police officer uses to stop traffic at an intersection. Hold the food treat in your right hand as before, but this time the food is not touching the dog's

Training Tip

When calling the dog, do not say 'Come.' Say things like, 'Rover, where are you? See if you can find me! I have a biscuit for you!' Keep up a constant line of chatter with coaxing sounds and frequent questions such as, 'Where are you?' The dog will learn to follow the sound of your voice to locate you and receive his reward.

these feelings to come through in the tone of his voice when he calls his dog. Hearing that desperation in his owner's voice, the dog fears the results of going to him and therefore either disobeys outright or runs in the opposite direction. The secret, therefore, is to teach the dog a game and, when you want him to come to you, simply play the game. It is practically a no-fail solution!

To begin, have several members of your family take a few food treats and each go into a different room in the house. Take turns calling the dog, and each person should celebrate the dog's finding him with a treat and lots of happy praise. When a person calls the dog, he is actually inviting the dog to find him and get a treat as a reward for 'winning.'

A few turns of the 'Where are you?' game and the dog will

An untrained Cairn can become very possessive of a toy and might bite your hand if you try to take it away from him. Start teaching your pup at an early age that your hand is NEVER to be attacked.

understand that everyone is playing the game and that each person has a big celebration awaiting his success at locating them. Once he learns to love the game, simply calling out 'Where are you?' will bring him running from wherever he is when he hears that all-important question.

The Come command is recognised as one of the most important things to teach a dog, but there are trainers who work with thousands of dogs and never teach the actual word 'Come.' Yet these dogs will race to respond to a person who uses the dog's name followed by 'Where are you?' For example, a woman has a 12-year-old companion dog who went blind, but who never fails to locate her owner when asked, 'Where are you?'

Children particularly love to

Training Tip

Never call your dog to come to you for a correction or scold him when he reaches you. That is the quickest way to turn a 'Come' command into 'Go away fast!' Dogs think only in the present tense, and your dog will connect the scolding with coming to you, not with the misbehaviour of a few moments earlier.

99

play this game with their dogs. Children can hide in smaller places like a shower or bath, behind a bed or under a table. The dog needs to work a little bit harder to find these hiding places, but when he does he loves to celebrate with a treat and a tussle with a favourite youngster.

TEACHING HEEL

Heeling means that the dog walks beside the owner without pulling. It takes time and patience on the owner's part to succeed at teaching the dog that he (the owner) will not proceed unless

Training Tip

Play fetch games with your puppy in an enclosed area where he can retrieve his toy and bring it back to you. Always use a toy or object

designated just for this purpose. Never use a shoe, stocking or other item he may later confuse with those in your closet or underneath your chair.

Training Tip

If you begin teaching the heel by taking long walks and letting the dog pull you along, he misinterprets this action as an acceptable form of taking a walk. When you pull back on the lead to counteract his pulling, he reads that tug as a signal to pull even harder!

the dog is walking calmly beside him. Pulling out ahead on the lead is definitely not acceptable.

Begin with holding the lead in your left hand as the dog sits beside your left leg. Move the loop end of the lead to your right hand but keep your left hand short on the lead so it keeps the dog in close next to you.

Say 'Heel' and step forward on your left foot. Keep the dog close to you and take three steps. Stop and have the dog sit next to you in what we now call the 'heel position.' Praise verbally, but do not touch the dog. Hesitate a moment and begin again with 'Heel,' taking three steps and stopping, at which point the dog is told to sit again.

Your goal here is to have the dog walk those three steps without pulling on the lead. When he will walk calmly beside you for three steps without pulling, increase the number of

Training Tip

Teach your dog to HEEL in an enclosed area. Once you think the dog will obey reliably and you want to attempt advanced obedience exercises such as off-lead heeling, test him in a fenced in area so he cannot run away.

Each time the dog looks up at you or slows down to give a slack lead between the two of you, quietly praise him and say, 'Good heel. Good dog.' Eventually, the dog will begin to respond and within a few days he will be walking politely beside you

You can hardly call your Cairn a pet unless he will walk comfortably at your side without constantly tugging on the lead. Heel training pays off on a daily basis!

steps you take to five. When he will walk politely beside you whilst you take five steps, you can increase the length of your walk to ten steps. Keep increasing the length of your stroll until the dog will walk quietly beside you without pulling as long as you want him to heel. When you stop heeling, indicate to the dog that the exercise is over by verbally praising as you pet him and say 'OK, good dog.' The 'OK' is used as a release word meaning that the exercise is finished and the dog is free to relax.

If you are dealing with a dog who insists on pulling you around, simply 'put on your brakes' and stand your ground until the dog realises that the two of you are not going anywhere until he is beside you and moving at your pace, not his. It may take some time just standing there to convince the dog that you are the leader and you will be the one to decide on the direction and speed of your travel.

Training Tip

If you are walking your dog and he suddenly stops and looks straight into your eyes, ignore him. Pull the leash and lead him into the direction you want to walk.

without pulling on the lead. At first, the training sessions should be kept short and very positive; soon the dog will be able to walk nicely with you for increasingly longer distances. Remember also to give the dog free time and the opportunity to run and play when you have finished heel practice.

WEANING OFF FOOD IN TRAINING

Food is used in training new behaviours. Once the dog understands what behaviour goes with a specific command, it is time to start weaning him off the food treats. At first, give a treat after each exercise. Then, start to give a treat only after every other

Obedience Class

A basic obedience beginner's class usually lasts for six to eight weeks. Dog and owner attend an hour-long lesson once a week and practise for a few minutes, several times a day, each day at home. If done properly, the whole procedure will result in a well-mannered dog and an owner who delights in living with a pet that is eager to please and enjoys doing things with his owner.

Did You Know?

If you have other pets in the home and/or interact often with the pets of friends and other family members, your pup will respond to those pets in much the same manner as you do. It is only when you show fear or resentment toward another animal that he will act fearful or unfriendly.

exercise. Mix up the times when you offer a food reward and the times when you only offer praise so that the dog will never know when he is going to receive both food and praise and when he is going to receive only praise. This is called a variable ratio reward system and it proves successful because there is always the chance that the owner will produce a treat, so the dog never stops trying for that reward. No matter what, ALWAYS give verbal praise.

OBEDIENCE CLASSES

It is a good idea to enrol in an obedience class if one is available in your area. If yours is a show dog, ringcraft classes would be more appropriate. Many areas have dog clubs that offer basic obedience training as well as preparatory classes for obedience competition. There are also local dog trainers who offer similar classes.

At obedience trials, dogs can earn titles at various levels of competition. The beginning levels of competition include basic behaviours such as sit, down, heel, etc. The more advanced levels of competition include jumping, retrieving, scent discrimination and signal work. The advanced levels require a dog and owner to put a lot of time and effort into their training and the titles that can be earned at these levels of competition are very prestigious.

OTHER ACTIVITIES FOR LIFE
Whether a dog is trained in the structured environment of a class or alone with his owner at home, there are many activities that can bring fun and rewards to both owner and dog once they have mastered basic control.

Teaching the dog to help out around the home, in the garden or on the farm provides great satisfaction to both dog and owner. In addition, the dog's help makes life a little easier for his owner and raises his stature as a valued companion to his family. It helps give the dog a purpose by occupying his mind and providing an outlet for his energy.

Backpacking is an exciting and healthy activity that the dog can be taught without assistance from more than his owner. The exercise of walking and climbing is good

for man and dog alike, and the bond that they develop together is priceless.

If you are interested in participating in organised competition with your Cairn Terrier, there are activities other than obedience in which you and your dog can become involved. Agility is a popular and fun sport where dogs run through an obstacle course that includes various jumps, tunnels and other exercises to test the dog's speed and coordination. The owners run through the course beside their dogs to give commands and to guide them through the course. Although competitive, the focus is on fun— it's fun to do, fun to watch, and great exercise.

Did You Know?

Occasionally, a dog and owner who have not attended formal classes have been able to earn entry-level titles by obtaining competition rules and regulations from a local kennel club and practising on their own to a degree of perfection. Obtaining the higher level titles, however, almost always requires extensive training under the tutelage of experienced instructors. In addition, the more difficult levels require more specialised equipment whereas the lower levels do not.

Internal Organs with Skeletal Structure

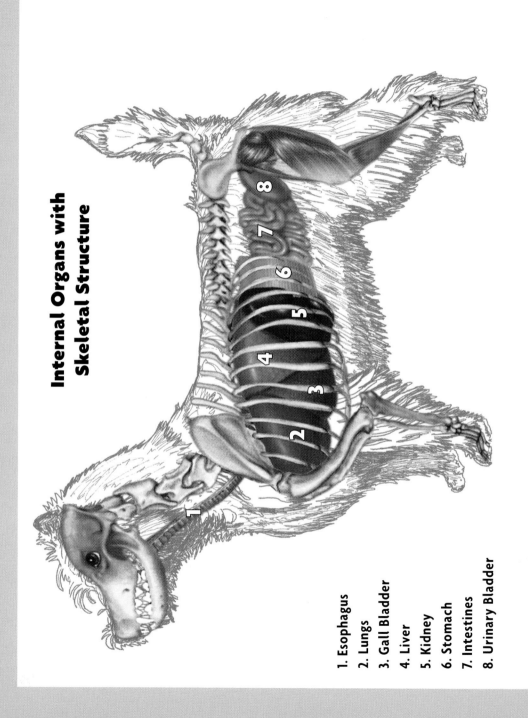

1. Esophagus
2. Lungs
3. Gall Bladder
4. Liver
5. Kidney
6. Stomach
7. Intestines
8. Urinary Bladder

Dogs suffer many of the same physical illnesses as people. They might even share many of the same psychological problems. Since people usually know more about human diseases than canine maladies, many of the terms used in this chapter will be familiar but not necessarily those used by veterinary surgeons. We will use the term *x-ray*, instead of the more acceptable term *radiograph*. We will also use the familiar term *symptoms* even though dogs don't have symptoms, which are verbal descriptions of the patient's feelings; dogs have *clinical signs*. Since dogs can't speak, we have to look for clinical signs...but we still use the term symptoms in this book.

As a general rule, medicine is practised. That term is not arbitrary. Medicine is a constantly changing art as we learn more and more about genetics, electronic aids (like CAT scans) and daily labora-

tory advances. There are many dog maladies, like canine hip dysplasia, which are not universally treated in the same manner. Some veterinary surgeons opt for surgery more often than others do.

SELECTING A VETERINARY SURGEON
Your selection of a veterinary surgeon should not be based upon personality (as most are) but upon their convenience to your home. You want a vet who is close because you might have emergencies or need to make multiple visits for treatments. You want a vet who has services that you might require, such as tattooing and grooming facilities, as well as sophisticated pet supplies and a good reputation for ability and responsiveness. There is nothing more frustrating than having to wait a day or more to get a response from your veterinary surgeon.

A qualified veterinary surgeon is able to provide your Cairn Terrier with all the care he requires, including recommendations for specialised testing and treatment.

A typical American vet's income categorised according to services performed. This survey dealt with small-animal (pet) practices.

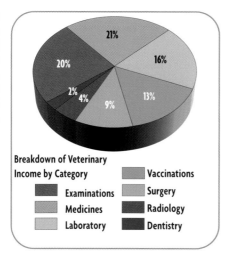

21%

16%

20%

2% 4%

9%

13%

Breakdown of Veterinary Income by Category

- Examinations
- Medicines
- Laboratory
- Vaccinations
- Surgery
- Radiology
- Dentistry

All veterinary surgeons are licensed and their diplomas and/or certificates should be displayed in their waiting rooms. There are, however, many veterinary specialities that usually require further studies and internships. There are specialists in heart problems (veterinary cardiologists), skin problems (veterinary dermatologists), teeth and gum problems (veterinary dentists), eye problems (veterinary ophthalmologists), X-rays (veterinary radiologists), and surgeons who have specialities in bones, muscles or other organs. Most veterinary surgeons do routine surgery such as neutering, stitching up wounds and docking tails for those breeds in which such is required for show purposes. When the problem affecting your dog is serious, it is not unusual or impudent to get another medical opinion, although in Britain you are obliged to advise the vets concerned about this. You might

Did You Know?

Your veterinary surgeon will probably recommend that your puppy be vaccinated before you take him outside. There are airborne diseases, parasite eggs in the grass and unexpected visits from other dogs that might be dangerous to your puppy's health.

also want to compare costs amongst several veterinary surgeons. Sophisticated health care and veterinary services can be very costly. Don't be bashful about discussing these costs with your veterinary surgeon or his (her) staff. It is not infrequent that important decisions are based upon financial considerations.

Did You Know?

Not every dog's ears are the same. Ears that are open to the air are healthier than ears with poor air circulation. Sometimes a dog can have two differently shaped ears. You should not probe inside your dog's ears. Only clean that which is accessible with a soft cotton wipe.

First Aid
at a Glance

Burns
Place the affected area under cool water;
use ice if only a small area is burnt.

Car accident
Move dog from roadway with blanket;
seek veterinary aid.

Bee/Insect bites
Apply ice to relieve swelling; antihista-
mine dosed properly.

Shock
Calm the dog, keep him warm; seek
immediate veterinary help.

Animal bites
Clean any bleeding area; apply pressure
until bleeding subsides; go to the vet.

Nosebleed
Apply cold compress to the nose; apply
pressure to any visible abrasion.

Spider bites
Use cold compress and a pressurised
pack to inhibit venom's spreading.

Bleeding
Apply pressure above the area; treat
wound by applying a cotton pack.

Antifreeze poisoning
Immediately induce vomiting by using
hydrogen peroxide.

Heat stroke
Submerge dog in cold bath; cool down
with fresh air and water; go to the vet.

Fish hooks
Removal best handled by vet;
hook must be cut in order to remove.

Frostbite/Hypothermia
Warm the dog with a warm bath, electric
blankets or hot water bottles.

Snake bites
Pack ice around bite; contact vet
quickly; identify snake for proper
antivenin.

Abrasions
Clean the wound and wash out
thoroughly with fresh water;
apply antiseptic.

 *Remember: an injured dog may attempt
to bite a helping hand from fear and confusion.
Always muzzle the dog before trying to offer assistance.*

PREVENTATIVE MEDICINE

It is much easier, less costly and more effective to practise preventative medicine than to fight bouts of illness and disease. Properly bred puppies come from parents that were selected based upon their genetic disease profile. Their mothers should have been vaccinated, free of all internal and

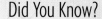

Did You Know?

Cases of hyperactive adrenal glands (Cushing's disease) have been traced to the drinking of highly chlorinated water. Aerate or age your dog's drinking water before offering it.

external parasites, and properly nourished. For these reasons, a visit to the veterinary surgeon who cared for the dam (mother) is recommended. The dam can pass on disease resistance to her puppies, which can last for eight to ten weeks. She can also pass on parasites and many infections. That's why you should visit the veterinary surgeon who cared for the dam.

Did You Know?

It was announced in April 1999 that the severe quarantine laws imposed on animals entering Britain from other rabies-free countries would become a thing of the past by April 2001. Rather than being confined to a kennel for six months upon arrival in Britain, animals undergo a series of blood tests and vaccinations, and are identifed by microchip implantation. Qualified pets receive a 'health passport' that allows their owners to travel with them in between Britain and other (mostly European) countries in which rabies does not exist.

Animals from countries such as the United States and Canada, where rabies is a problem, still will be subject to quarantine. Although veterinary standards are high in these countries, recently infected dogs may test negative to the disease and, without the quarantine period, may unknowingly introduce rabies into previously unaffected countries.

WEANING TO FIVE MONTHS OLD

Puppies should be weaned by the time they are about two months old. A puppy that remains for at least eight weeks with its mother and littermates usually adapts better to other dogs and people later in its life.

Some new owners have their puppy examined by a veterinary surgeon immediately, which is a good idea. Vaccination programmes usually begin when the puppy is very young.

The puppy will have its teeth examined and have its skeletal conformation and general health

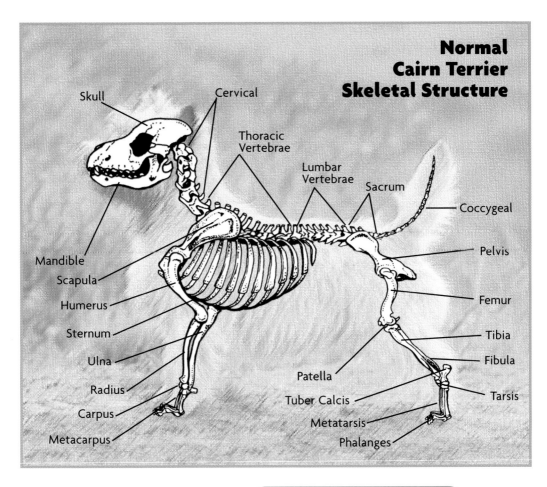

Normal Cairn Terrier Skeletal Structure

Skull
Cervical
Thoracic Vertebrae
Lumbar Vertebrae
Sacrum
Coccygeal
Pelvis
Mandible
Scapula
Humerus
Sternum
Ulna
Radius
Carpus
Metacarpus
Femur
Tibia
Fibula
Patella
Tuber Calcis
Metatarsis
Phalanges
Tarsis

checked prior to certification by the veterinary surgeon. Puppies in certain breeds have problems with their kneecaps, eye cataracts and other eye problems, heart murmurs and undescended testicles. They may also have personality problems and your veterinary surgeon might have training in temperament evaluation.

VACCINATION SCHEDULING
Most vaccinations are given by injection and should only be done

Did You Know?

Dogs who have been exposed to lawns sprayed with herbicides have double and triple the rate of malignant lymphoma. Town dogs are especially at risk, as they are exposed to tailored lawns and gardens. Dogs perspire and absorb through their footpads. Be careful where your dog walks and always avoid any area that appears yellowed from chemical overspray.

HEALTH AND VACCINATION SCHEDULE

AGE IN WEEKS:	3RD	6TH	8TH	10TH	12TH	14TH	16TH	20-24TH
Worm Control	✔	✔	✔	✔	✔	✔	✔	✔
Neutering								✔
Heartworm*		✔						✔
Parvovirus		✔		✔		✔		✔
Distemper			✔		✔		✔	
Hepatitis			✔		✔		✔	
Leptospirosis		✔		✔		✔		
Parainfluenza		✔		✔		✔		
Dental Examination			✔					✔
Complete Physical			✔					✔
Temperament Testing			✔					
Coronavirus					✔			
Kennel Cough		✔						
Hip Dysplasia							✔	
Rabies*								✔

Vaccinations are not instantly effective. It takes about two weeks for the dog's immunisation system to develop antibodies. Most vaccinations require annual booster shots. Your veterinary surgeon should guide you in this regard.
*Not applicable in the United Kingdom

by a veterinary surgeon. Both he and you should keep a record of the date of the injection, the identification of the vaccine and the amount given. Some vets give a first vaccination at eight weeks, but most dog breeders prefer the course not to commence until about ten weeks because of negating any antibodies passed on by the dam. The vaccination scheduling is usually based on a 15-day cycle. You must take your vet's advice as to when to vaccinate as this may differ

Did You Know?

Vaccines do not work all the time. Sometimes dogs are allergic to them and many times the antibodies, which are supposed to be stimulated by the vaccine, just are not produced. You should keep your dog in the veterinary clinic for an hour after it is vaccinated to be sure there are no allergic reactions.

Did You Know?

Male dogs are neutered. The operation removes the testicles and requires that the dog be anaesthetised. Recovery takes about one week. Females are spayed. This is major surgery and it usually takes a bitch two weeks to recover.

according to the vaccine used. Most vaccinations immunise your puppy against viruses.

The usual vaccines contain immunising doses of several different viruses such as distemper, parvovirus, parainfluenza and hepatitis. There are other vaccines available when the puppy is at risk. You should rely upon professional

When you take your Cairn puppy home from the breeder, you should immediately visit your veterinary surgeon to discuss your dog's present and future needs and to have your new puppy evaluated for possible health concerns.

advice. This is especially true for the booster-shot programme. Most vaccination programmes require a booster when the puppy is a year old and once a year thereafter. In some cases, circumstances may require more frequent immunisations. Kennel cough, more formally known as tracheobronchitis, is treated with a vaccine that is sprayed into the dog's nostrils. Kennel cough is usually included in routine vaccination, but this is often not so effective as for other major diseases.

FIVE MONTHS TO ONE YEAR OF AGE
Unless you intend to breed or show your dog, neutering the puppy at six months of age is

> ## Did You Know?
>
> Feeding your dog properly is very important. An incorrect diet could affect the dog's health, behaviour and nervous system, possibly making a normal dog into an aggressive one.

recommended. Discuss this with your veterinary surgeon; most professionals advise neutering the puppy. Neutering has proven to be extremely beneficial to both male and female puppies. Besides eliminating the possibility of pregnancy, it inhibits (but does not prevent) breast cancer in bitches and prostate cancer in

Disease	What is it?	What causes it?	Symptoms
Leptospirosis	Severe disease that affects the internal organs; can be spread to people.	A bacterium, which is often carried by rodents, that enters through mucous membranes and spreads quickly throughout the body.	Range from fever, vomiting and loss of appetite in less severe cases to shock, irreversible kidney damage and possibly death in most severe cases.
Rabies	Potentially deadly virus that infects warm-blooded mammals. Not seen in United Kingdom.	Bite from a carrier of the virus, mainly wild animals.	1st stage: dog exhibits change in behaviour, fear. 2nd stage: dog's behaviour becomes more aggressive. 3rd stage: loss of coordination, trouble with bodily functions.
Parvovirus	Highly contagious virus, potentially deadly.	Ingestion of the virus, which is usually spread through the faeces of infected dogs.	Most common: severe diarrhoea. Also vomiting, fatigue, lack of appetite.
Kennel cough	Contagious respiratory infection.	Combination of types of bacteria and virus. Most common: *Bordetella bronchiseptica* bacteria and parainfluenza virus.	Chronic cough.
Distemper	Disease primarily affecting respiratory and nervous system.	Virus that is related to the human measles virus.	Mild symptoms such as fever, lack of appetite and mucous secretion progress to evidence of brain damage, 'hard pad.'
Hepatitis	Virus primarily affecting the liver.	Canine adenovirus type I (CAV-1). Enters system when dog breathes in particles.	Lesser symptoms include listlessness, diarrhoea, vomiting. More severe symptoms include 'blue-eye' (clumps of virus in eye).
Coronavirus	Virus resulting in digestive problems.	Virus is spread through infected dog's faeces.	Stomach upset evidenced by lack of appetite, vomiting, diarrhoea.

male dogs. Under no circumstances should a bitch be spayed prior to her first season.

DOGS OLDER THAN ONE YEAR
Continue to visit the veterinary surgeon at least once a year. There is no such disease as old age, but bodily functions do change with age. The eyes and ears are no longer as efficient. Liver, kidney and intestinal functions often decline. Proper dietary changes, recommended by your veterinary surgeon, can make life more pleasant for the ageing Cairn Terrier and you.

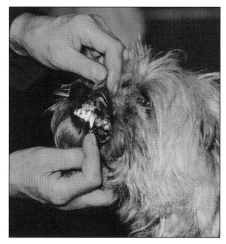

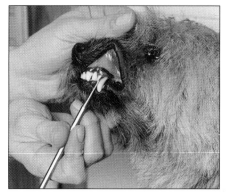

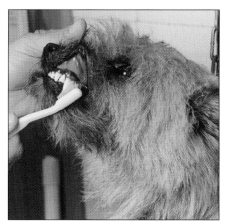

Your Cairn's well being depends on his healthy teeth. Keep a close eye on his teeth and gums. Brush the teeth regularly. Cleaning is the owner's responsibility unless you prefer to have your vet scale the teeth, remove plaque and polish the teeth. Your veterinary surgeon usually puts the dog to sleep for this procedure.

Did You Know?

A dental examination is in order when the dog is between six months and one year of age so any permanent teeth that have erupted incorrectly can be corrected. It is important to begin a brushing routine, preferably using a two-sided brushing technique, whereby both sides of the tooth are brushed at the same time. Durable nylon and safe edible chews should be a part of your puppy's arsenal for good health, good teeth and pleasant breath. The vast majority of dogs three to four years old and older has diseases of the gums from lack of dental attention. Using the various types of dental chews can be very effective in controlling dental plaque.

Did You Know?

Chances are that you and your dog will have the same allergies. Your allergies are readily recognisable and usually easily treated. Your dog's allergies may be masked.

SKIN PROBLEMS IN CAIRN TERRIERS

Veterinary surgeons are consulted by dog owners for skin problems more than any other group of diseases or maladies. Dogs' skin is almost as sensitive as human skin and both suffer almost the same ailments (though the occurrence of acne in dogs is rare!). For this reason, veterinary dermatology has developed into a speciality practised by many veterinary surgeons.

Since many skin problems have visual symptoms that are almost identical, it requires the skill of an experienced veterinary dermatologist to identify and cure many of the more severe skin disorders. Pet shops sell many treatments for skin problems but most of the treatments are directed at symptoms and not the underlying problem(s). If your dog is suffering from a skin disorder, you should seek professional assistance as quickly as possible. As with all diseases, the earlier a problem is identified and treated, the more successful is the cure.

INHERITED SKIN PROBLEMS

Many skin disorders are inherited and some are fatal. For example, acrodermatitis is an inherited disease that is transmitted by both parents. The parents, who appear (phenotypically) normal, have a recessive gene for acrodermatitis, meaning that they carry, but are not affected by the disease.

Acrodermatitis is just one example of how difficult it is to prevent congenital dog diseases. The cost and skills required to ascertain whether two dogs should be mated are too high even though puppies with acrodermatitis rarely reach two years of age.

Other inherited skin problems are usually not as fatal as acrodermatitis. All inherited diseases must be diagnosed and treated by

Did You Know?

You are your dog's caretaker and his dentist. Vets warn that plaque and tartar buildup on the teeth will damage the gums and allow bacteria to enter the dog's bloodstream, causing serious damage to the animal's vital organs. Studies show that over 50 percent of dogs have some form of gum disease before age three. Daily or weekly tooth cleaning (with a brush or soft gauze pad wipes) can add years to your dog's life.

a veterinary specialist. There are active programmes being undertaken by many veterinary pharmaceutical manufacturers to solve most, if not all, of the common skin problems of dogs.

PARASITE BITES

Many of us are allergic to insect bites. The bites itch, erupt and may even become infected. Dogs have the same reaction to fleas, ticks and/or mites. When an insect lands on you, you have the chance to whisk it away with your hand. Unfortunately, when our dog is bitten by a flea, tick or mite, it can only scratch it away or bite it. By the time the dog has been bitten, the parasite has done some of its damage. It may also have laid eggs to cause further problems in the near future. The itching from parasite bites is probably due to the saliva injected into the site when the parasite sucks the dog's blood.

Did You Know?

Never allow your dog to swim in polluted water or public areas where water quality can be suspect. Even perfectly clear water can harbour parasites, many of which can cause serious to fatal illnesses in canines. Areas inhabited by waterfowl and other wildlife are especially dangerous.

AUTO-IMMUNE SKIN CONDITIONS

Auto-immune skin conditions are commonly referred to as being allergic to yourself, whilst allergies are usually inflammatory reactions to an outside stimulus. Auto-immune diseases cause serious damage to the tissues that are involved.

The best known auto-immune disease is lupus, which affects people as well as dogs. The symptoms are variable and may affect the kidneys, bones, blood chemistry and skin. It can be fatal to both dogs and humans, though it is not thought to be transmissible. It is usually successfully treated with cortisone, prednisone or similar corticosteroid, but extensive use of these drugs can have harmful side effects.

AIRBORNE ALLERGIES

An interesting allergy is pollen allergy. Humans have hay fever, rose fever and other fevers with which they suffer during the pollinating season. Many dogs suffer the same allergies. When the pollen count is high, your dog might suffer but don't expect them to sneeze and have runny noses like humans. Dogs react to pollen allergies the same way they react to fleas—they scratch and bite themselves.

Dogs, like humans, can be tested for allergens. Discuss the testing with your veterinary dermatologist.

FOOD PROBLEMS

FOOD ALLERGIES

Dogs are allergic to many foods that are best-sellers and highly recommended by breeders and veterinary surgeons. Changing the brand of food that you buy may not eliminate the problem if the element to which the dog is allergic is contained in the new brand.

Recognising a food allergy is difficult. Humans vomit or have rashes when they eat a food to which they are allergic. Dogs neither vomit nor (usually) develop a rash. They react in the same manner as they do to an airborne or flea allergy: they itch, scratch and bite. Thus making the diagnosis extremely difficult. Whilst pollen allergies and parasite bites are usually seasonal, food allergies are year-round problems.

FOOD INTOLERANCE

Food intolerance is the inability of the dog to completely digest certain foods. Puppies that may have done very well on their mother's milk may not do well on cow's milk. The result of this food intolerance may be loose bowels, passing gas and stomach pains. These are the only obvious symptoms of food intolerance and that makes diagnosis difficult.

TREATING FOOD PROBLEMS

It is possible to handle food allergies and food intolerance yourself. Put your dog on a diet that it has never had. Obviously if it has never eaten this new food it can't have been allergic or intolerant of it. Start with a single ingredient that is not in the dog's diet at the present time. Ingredients like chopped beef or fish are common in dog's diets, so try something more exotic like rabbit, pheasant or even just vegetables. Keep the dog on this diet (with no additives) for a month. If the symptoms of food allergy or intolerance disappear, chances are your dog has a food allergy.

Don't think that the single ingredient cured the problem. You

Keep 'people food' out of your Cairn's reach. No dog can resist stealing a tasty morsel, but these 'treats' can give your pet an upset stomach.

still must find a suitable diet and ascertain which ingredient in the old diet was objectionable. This is most easily done by adding ingredients to the new diet one at a time. Let the dog stay on the modified diet for a month before you add another ingredient. Eventually, you will determine the ingredient that caused the adverse reaction.

An alternative method is to carefully study the ingredients in the diet to which your dog is allergic or intolerant. Identify the main ingredient in this diet and eliminate the main ingredient by buying a different food that does not have that ingredient. Keep experimenting until the symptoms disappear after one month on the new diet.

117

HOMEOPATHY:
an alternative to medicine

'Less is Most'

Using this principle, the strength of a homeopathic remedy is measured by the number of serial dilutions that were undertaken to create it. The greater the number of serial dilutions, the greater the strength of the homeopathic remedy. The potency of a remedy that has been made by making a dilution of 1 part in 100 parts (or 1/100) is 1c or 1cH. If this remedy is subjected to a series of further dilutions, each one being 1/100, a more dilute and stronger remedy is produced. If the remedy is diluted in this way six times, it is called 6c or 6cH. A dilution of 6c is 1 part in 1000,000,000,000. In general, higher potencies in more frequent doses are better for acute symptoms and lower potencies in more infrequent doses are more useful for chronic, long-standing problems.

CURING OUR DOGS NATURALLY

Holistic medicine means treating the whole animal as a unique, perfect living being. Generally, holistic treatments do not suppress the symptoms that the body naturally produces, as do most medications prescribed by conventional doctors and vets. Holistic methods seek to cure disease by regaining balance and harmony in the patient's environment. Some of these methods include use of nutritional therapy, herbs, flower essences, aromatherapy, acupuncture, massage, chiropractic, and, of course the most popular holistic approach, homeopathy. Homeopathy is a theory or system of treating illness with small doses of substances which, if administered in larger quantities, would produce the symptoms that the patient already has. This approach is often described as 'like cures like.' Although modern veterinary medicine is geared toward the 'quick fix,' homeopathy relies on the belief that, given the time, the body is able to heal itself and return to its natural, healthy state.

Choosing a remedy to cure a problem in our dogs is the difficult part of homeopathy. Consult with your veterinary surgeon for a professional diagnosis of your dog's symptoms. Often these symptoms require immediate conventional

care. If your vet is willing, and somewhat knowledgeable, you may attempt a homeopathic remedy. Be aware that cortisone prevents homeopathic remedies from working. There are hundreds of possibilities and combinations to cure many problems in dogs, from basic physical problems such as excessive moulting, fleas or other parasites, unattractive doggy odour, bad breath, upset tummy, dry, oily or dull coat, diarrhoea, ear problems or eye discharge (including tears and dry or mucousy matter), to behavioural abnormalities, such as fear of loud noises, habitual licking, poor appetite, excessive barking, obesity and various phobias. From alumina to zincum metallicum, the remedies span the planet and the imagination…from flowers and weeds to chemicals, insect droppings, diesel smoke and volcanic ash.

Using 'Like to Treat Like'

Unlike conventional medicines that suppress symptoms, homeopathic remedies treat illnesses with small doses of substances that, if administered in larger quantities, would produce the symptoms that the patient already has. Whilst the same homeopathic remedy can be used to treat different symptoms in different dogs, here are some interesting remedies and their uses.

Apis Mellifica
(made from honey bee venom) can be used for allergies or to reduce swelling that occurs in acutely infected kidneys.

Diesel Smoke
can be used to help control travel sickness.

Calcarea Fluorica
(made from calcium fluoride which helps harden bone structure) can be useful in treating hard lumps in tissues.

Natrum Muriaticum
(made from common salt, sodium chloride) is useful in treating thin, thirsty dogs.

Nitricum Acidum
(made from nitric acid) is used for symptoms you would expect to see from contact with acids such as lesions, especially where the skin joins the linings of body orifices or openings such as the lips and nostrils.

Symphytum
(made from the herb Knitbone, Symphytum officianale) is used to encourage bones to heal.

Urtica Urens
(made from the common stinging nettle) is used in treating painful, irritating rashes.

119

HOMEOPATHIC REMEDIES FOR YOUR DOG

Symptom/Ailment	Possible Remedy
ALLERGIES	Apis Mellifica 30c, Astacus Fluviatilis 6c, Pulsatilla 30c, Urtica Urens 6c
ALOPECIA	Alumina 30c, Lycopodium 30c, Sepia 30c, Thallium 6c
ANAL GLANDS (BLOCKED)	Hepar Sulphuris Calcareum 30c, Sanicula 6c, Silicea 6c
ARTHRITIS	Rhus Toxicodendron 6c, Bryonia Alba 6c
CATARACT	Calcarea Carbonica 6c, Conium Maculatum 6c, Phosphorus 30c, Silicea 30c
CONSTIPATION	Alumina 6c, Carbo Vegetabilis 30c, Graphites 6c, Nitricum Acidum 30c, Silicea 6c
COUGHING	Aconitum Napellus 6c, Belladonna 30c, Hyoscyamus Niger 30c, Phosphorus 30c
DIARRHOEA	Arsenicum Album 30c, Aconitum Napellus 6c, Chamomilla 30c, Mercurius Corrosivus 30c
DRY EYE	Zincum Metallicum 30c
EAR PROBLEMS	Aconitum Napellus 30c, Belladonna 30c, Hepar Sulphuris 30c, Tellurium 30c, Psorinum 200c
EYE PROBLEMS	Borax 6c, Aconitum Napellus 30c, Graphites 6c, Staphysagria 6c, Thuja Occidentalis 30c
GLAUCOMA	Aconitum Napellus 30c, Apis Mellifica 6c, Phosphorus 30c
HEAT STROKE	Belladonna 30c, Gelsemium Sempervirens 30c, Sulphur 30c
HICCOUGHS	Cinchona Deficinalis 6c
HIP DYSPLASIA	Colocynthis 6c, Rhus Toxicodendron 6c, Bryonia Alba 6c
INCONTINENCE	Argentum Nitricum 6c, Causticum 30c, Conium Maculatum 30c, Pulsatilla 30c, Sepia 30c
INSECT BITES	Apis Mellifica 30c, Cantharis 30c, Hypericum Perforatum 6c, Urtica Urens 30c
ITCHING	Alumina 30c, Arsenicum Album 30c, Carbo Vegetabilis 30c, Hypericum Perforatum 6c, Mezerium 6c, Sulphur 30c
KENNEL COUGH	Drosera 6c, Ipecacuanha 30c
MASTITIS	Apis Mellifica 30c, Belladonna 30c, Urtica Urens 1m
PATELLAR LUXATION	Gelsemium Sempervirens 6c, Rhus Toxicodendron 6c
PENIS PROBLEMS	Aconitum Napellus 30c, Hepar Sulphuris Calcareum 30c, Pulsatilla 30c, Thuja Occidentalis 6c
PUPPY TEETHING	Calcarea Carbonica 6c, Chamomilla 6c, Phytolacca 6c
TRAVEL SICKNESS	Cocculus 6c, Petroleum 6c

The hairs of a Cairn Terrier. These are healthy hairs with intact cuticles (outer cover). This scanning electron micrograph (S.E.M.) has enlarged the hairs to 350 times the natural size.

S. E. M. by Dr Dennis Kunkel, University of Hawaii

A scanning electron micrograph (S. E. M.) of a dog flea, *Ctenocephalides canis*.

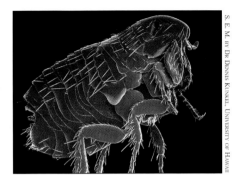

S. E. M. BY DR DENNIS KUNKEL, UNIVERSITY OF HAWAII

inside the body are a bit more difficult to eradicate but they are easier to control.

FLEAS

To control a flea infestation you have to understand the flea's life cycle. Fleas are often thought of as a summertime problem but centrally heated homes have changed the patterns and fleas can be found at any time of the year. The most effective method of flea control is a two-stage approach: one stage to kill the adult fleas, and the other to control the development of pre-adult fleas. Unfortunately, no single active ingredient is effective against all stages of the life cycle.

EXTERNAL PARASITES

Of all the problems to which dogs are prone, none is more well known and frustrating than fleas. Flea infestation is relatively simple to cure but difficult to prevent. Parasites that are harboured

Opposite page: A scanning electron micrograph of a dog or cat flea, *Ctenocephalides*, magnified more than 100x. This has been colourised for effect.

LIFE CYCLE STAGES

During its life, a flea will pass through four life stages: egg, larva, pupa and adult. The adult stage is the most visible and irritating stage of the flea life

Magnified head of a dog flea, *Ctenocephalides canis*.

Did You Know?

Fleas have been around for millions of years and have adapted to changing host animals.

They are able to go through a complete life cycle in less than one month or they can extend their lives to almost two years by remaining as pupae or cocoons. They do not need blood or any other food for up to 20 months.

They have been measured as being able to jump 300,000 times and can jump 150 times their length in any direction including straight up. Those are just a few of the reasons they are so successful in infesting a dog!

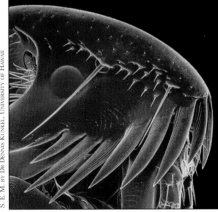

S. E. M. BY DR DENNIS KUNKEL, UNIVERSITY OF HAWAII

S. E. M. BY DR DENNIS KUNKEL, UNIVERSITY OF HAWAII

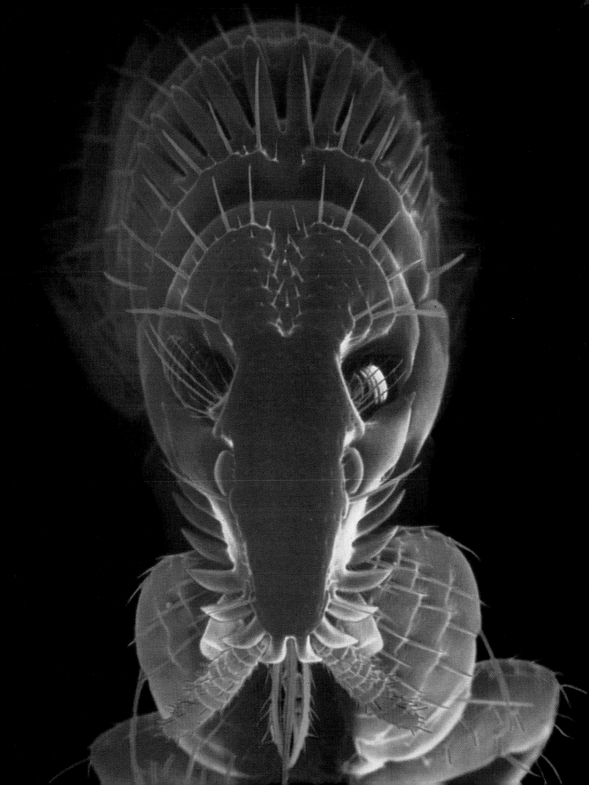

The Life Cycle of the Flea

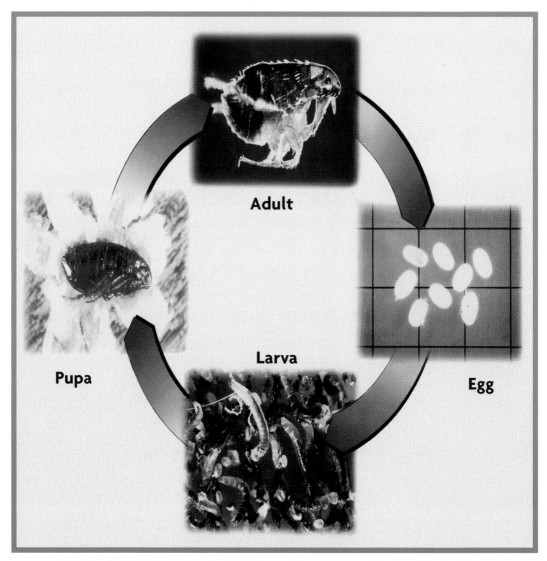

Adult

Pupa

Larva

Egg

The life cycle of the flea was posterised by Fleabusters˙. Poster courtesy of Fleabusters˙, R_x for Fleas.

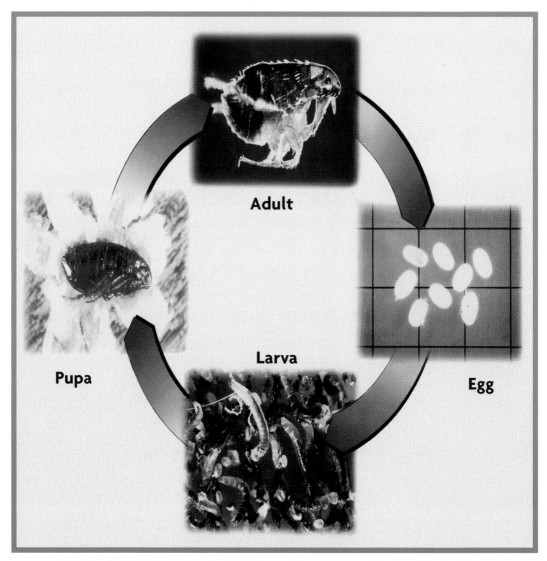

cycle and this is why the majority of flea-control products concentrate on this stage. The fact is that adult fleas account for only 1% of the total flea population, and the other 99% exist in pre-adult stages, i.e., eggs, larvae and pupae. The pre-adult stages are barely visible to the naked eye.

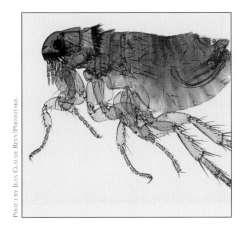

PHOTO BY JEAN CLAUDE REVY/PHOTOTAKE.

THE LIFE CYCLE OF THE FLEA

Eggs are laid on the dog, usually in quantities of about 20 or 30, several times a day. The female adult flea must have a blood meal before each egg-laying session. When first laid, the eggs will cling to the dog's fur, as the eggs are still moist. However, they will quickly dry out and fall from the dog, especially if the dog moves around or scratches. Many eggs will fall off in the dog's favourite area or an area in which

On Guard: Catching Fleas Off Guard

Consider the following ways to arm yourself against fleas:
• Add a small amount of pennyroyal or eucalyptus oil to your dog's bath. These natural remedies repel fleas.
• Supplement your dog's food with fresh garlic (minced or grated) and a hearty amount of brewer's yeast, both of which ward off fleas.
• Use a flea comb on your dog daily. Submerge fleas in a cup of bleach to kill them quickly.
• Confine the dog to only a few rooms to limit the spread of fleas in the home.
• Vacuum daily...and get all of the crevices! Dispose of the bag every few days until the problem is under control.
• Wash your dog's bedding daily. Cover cushions where your dog sleeps with towels, and wash the towels often.

A male dog flea, *Ctenocephalides canis.*

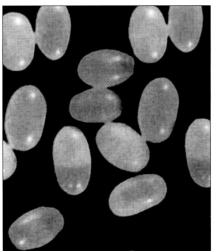

The eggs of the dog flea.

Male cat fleas, *Ctenocephalides felis*, are very commonly found on dogs.

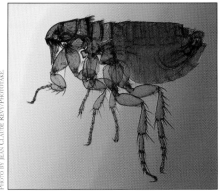

PHOTO BY JEAN CLAUDE REVY/PHOTOTAKE.

he spends a lot of time, such as his bed.

Once the eggs fall from the dog onto the carpet or furniture, they will hatch into larvae. This takes from one to ten days. Larvae are not particularly mobile, and will usually travel only a few inches from where they hatch. However, they do have a tendency to move away from light and heavy traffic—under furniture and behind doors are common places to find high quantities of flea larvae.

The flea larvae feed on dead organic matter, including adult flea faeces, until they are ready to change into adult fleas. Fleas will usually remain as larvae for around seven days. After this period, the larvae will pupate into protective pupae. While inside the pupae, the larvae will undergo metamorphosis and change into

PHOTO BY DWIGHT R KUHN.

adult fleas. This can take as little time as a few days, but the adult fleas can remain inside the pupae waiting to hatch for up to two years. The pupae are signalled to hatch by certain stimuli, such as physical pressure—the pupae's being stepped on, heat from an animal lying on the pupae or increased carbon dioxide levels and vibrations—indicating that a suitable host is available.

Once hatched, the adult flea must feed within a few days. Once the adult flea finds a host, it will not leave voluntarily. It only becomes dislodged by grooming or the host animal's scratching. The adult flea will remain on the host for the duration of its life unless forcibly removed.

TREATING THE ENVIRONMENT AND THE DOG

Treating fleas should be a two-pronged attack. First, the environment needs to be treated; this includes carpets and furniture,

PHOTO BY DWIGHT R KUHN.

Did You Know?

Never mix flea control products without first consulting your veterinary surgeon. Some products can become toxic when combined with others and can cause serious or fatal consequences.

especially the dog's bedding and areas underneath furniture. The environment should be treated with a household spray containing an Insect Growth Regulator (IGR) and an insecticide to kill the adult fleas. Most IGRs are effective against eggs and larvae; they actually mimic the fleas' own hormones and stop the eggs and larvae from developing into adult fleas. There are currently no treatments available to attack the pupa stage of the life cycle, so the adult insecticide is used to kill the newly hatched adult fleas before they find a host. Most IGRs are active for many months, whilst adult insecticides are only active for a few days.

When treating with a household spray, it is a good idea to vacuum before applying the product. This stimulates as many pupae as possible to hatch into adult fleas. The vacuum cleaner should also be treated with a flea treatment to prevent the eggs and larvae that have been hoovered into the vacuum bag from hatching.

The second stage of treatment is to apply an adult insecticide to the dog. Traditionally, this would be in the form of a collar or a spray, but more recent innovations include digestible insecticides that poison the fleas when they ingest the dog's blood. Alternatively, there are drops that, when placed on the back of the animal's neck, spread throughout the fur and skin to kill adult fleas.

Did You Know?

Two types of products should be used when treating fleas—a product to treat the pet and a product to treat the home. Adult fleas represent less than 1% of the flea population. The pre-adult fleas (eggs, larvae and pupae) represent more than 99% of the flea population and are found in the environment; it is in the case of pre-adult fleas that products containing an Insect Growth Regulator (IGR) should be used in the home.

IGRs are a new class of compounds used to prevent the development of insects. They do not kill the insect outright, but instead use the insect's biology against it to stop it from completing its growth. Products that contain methoprene are the world's first and leading IGRs. Used to control fleas and other insects, this type of IGR will stop flea larvae from developing and protect the house for up to seven months.

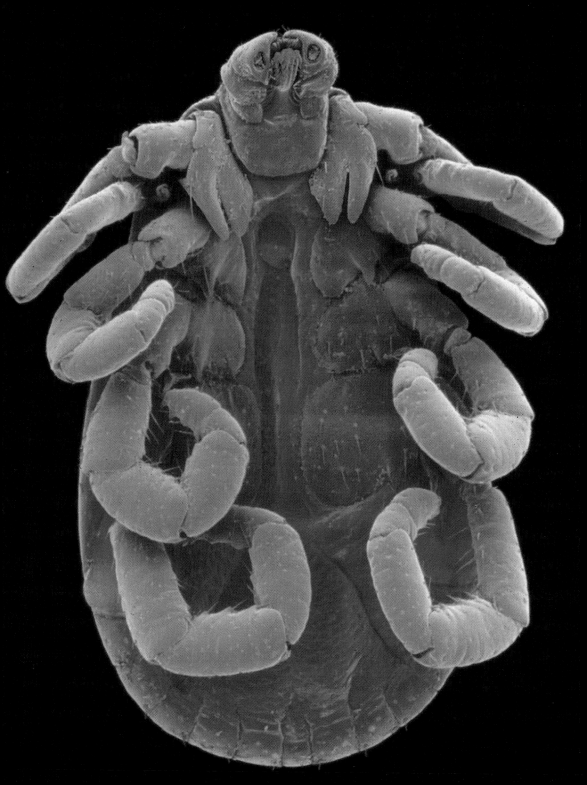

TICKS AND MITES

Though not as common as fleas, ticks and mites are found all over the tropical and temperate world. They don't bite, like fleas; they harpoon. They dig their sharp proboscis (nose) into the dog's skin and drink the blood. Their only food and drink is dog's blood. Dogs can get Lyme disease, Rocky Mountain spotted fever (normally found in the USA only), paralysis and many other diseases from ticks and mites. They may live where fleas are found and they like to hide in cracks or seams in walls wherever dogs live. They are controlled the same way fleas are controlled.

The dog tick, *Dermacentor variabilis*, may well be the most common dog tick in many geographical areas, especially those areas where the climate is hot and humid.

PHOTO BY JEAN CLAUDE REVY/PHOTOTAKE

An uncommon dog tick of the genus *Ixode*. Magnified 10x.

Opposite page: The dog tick, *Dermacentor variabilis*, is probably the most common tick found on dogs. Look at the strength in its eight legs! No wonder it's hard to detach them.

Most dog ticks have life expectancies of a week to six months, depending upon climatic conditions. They can neither jump nor fly, but they can crawl slowly and can range up to 5 metres (16 feet) to reach a sleeping or unsuspecting dog.

MANGE

Mites cause a skin irritation called mange. Some are contagious, like *Cheyletiella*, ear mites, scabies and chiggers. The non-contagious mites are *Demodex*. Mites that cause ear-mite infestation are usually controlled with ivermectin, which is often toxic to Collies and probably should be avoided in all herding breeds.

It is essential that your dog be treated for mange as quickly as possible because some forms of mange are transmissible to people.

A brown dog tick, *Rhipicephalus sanguineus*, is an uncommon but annoying tick found on dogs.

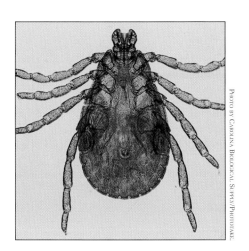

S. E. M. BY DR DENNIS KUNKEL, UNIVERSITY OF HAWAII

PHOTO BY CAROLINA BIOLOGICAL SUPPLY/PHOTOTAKE

129

Cairn Terrier

Two views of the mange mite, *Psoroptes bovis.*

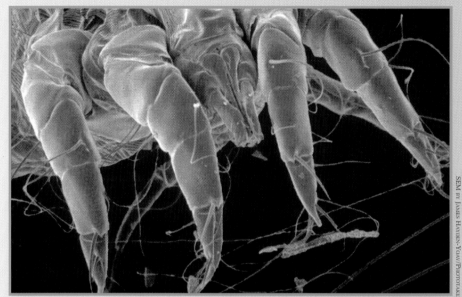

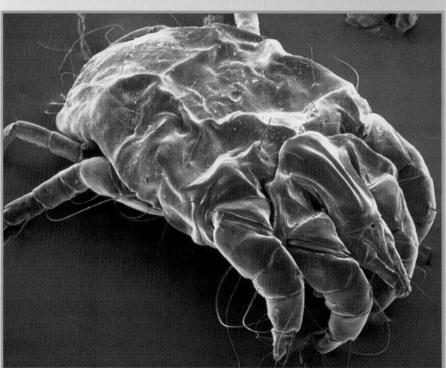

INTERNAL PARASITES

Most animals—fishes, birds and mammals, including dogs and humans—have worms and other parasites that live inside their bodies. According to Dr Herbert R Axelrod, the fish pathologist, there are two kinds of parasites: dumb and smart. The smart parasites live in peaceful cooperation with their hosts (symbiosis), while the dumb parasites kill their host. Most of the worm infections are relatively easy to control. If they are not controlled they eventually weaken the host dog to the point that other medical problems occur, but they are not dumb parasites.

ROUNDWORMS

The roundworms that infect dogs are scientifically known as *Toxocara canis*. They live in the dog's intestine. The worms shed eggs continually. It has been estimated that a dog produces about 150 grammes of faeces every day. Each gramme of faeces averages 10,000–12,000 eggs of roundworms. There are no known areas in which dogs roam that do not contain roundworm eggs. The greatest danger of roundworms is

> ## Did You Know?
>
> Ridding your puppy of worms is VERY IMPORTANT because certain worms that puppies carry, such as tapeworms and roundworms, can infect humans.
>
> Breeders initiate a deworming programme at or about four weeks of age. The routine is repeated every two or three weeks until the puppy is three months old. The breeder from whom you obtained your puppy should provide you with the complete details of the deworming programme.
>
> Your veterinary surgeon can prescribe and monitor the programme of deworming for you. The usual programme is treating the puppy every 15–20 days until the puppy is positively worm free.
>
> It is not advised that you treat your puppy with drugs that are not recommended professionally.

PHOTO BY CAROLINA BIOLOGICAL SUPPLY/PHOTOTAKE.

The roundworm, *Rhabditis*. The roundworm can infect both dogs and humans.

131

The roundworm *Rhabditis*.

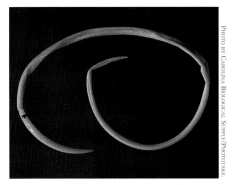

Photo by Carolina Biological Supply/Phototake.

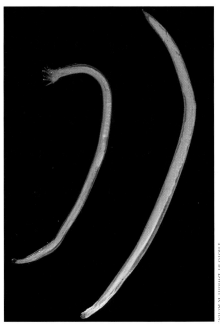

Photo by Dwight R Kuhn.

Male and female hookworms, *Ancylostoma caninum*, are uncommonly found in pet or show dogs in Britain. Hookworms may infect other dogs that have exposure to grasslands.

that they infect people too! It is wise to have your dog tested regularly for roundworms.

Pigs also have roundworm infections that can be passed to humans and dogs. The typical roundworm parasite is called *Ascaris lumbricoides*.

HOOKWORMS

The worm *Ancylostoma caninum* is commonly called the dog hookworm. It is dangerous to humans and cats. It also has teeth

Did You Know?

Caring for the puppy starts before the puppy is born by keeping the dam healthy and well-nourished. Most puppies have worms, even if they are not evident, so a worming programme is essential. The worms continually shed eggs except during their dormant stage, when they just rest in the tissues of the puppy. During this stage they are not evident during a routine examination.

by which it attaches itself to the intestines of the dog. It changes the site of its attachment about six times a day and the dog loses blood from each detachment, possibly causing iron-deficiency anaemia. Hookworms are easily purged from the dog with many medications. Milbemycin oxime, which also serves as a heartworm preventative in Collies, can be used for this purpose.

In Britain the 'temperate climate' hookworm (*Uncinaria stenocephala*) is rarely found in pet or show dogs, but can occur in hunting packs, racing Greyhounds and sheepdogs because the worms can be prevalent wherever dogs are exercised regularly on grassland.

Did You Know?

Average size dogs can pass 1,360,000 roundworm eggs every day.

For example, if there were only 1 million dogs in the world, the world would be saturated with 1,300 metric tonnes of dog faeces.

These faeces would contain 15,000,000,000 roundworm eggs.

7–31% of home gardens and children's play boxes in the U. S. contain roundworm eggs.

Flushing dog's faeces down the toilet is not a safe practice because the usual sewage treatments do not destroy roundworm eggs.

Infected puppies start shedding roundworm eggs at 3 weeks of age. They can be infected by their mother's milk.

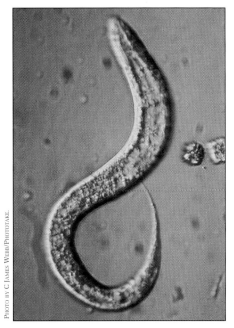

PHOTO BY C JAMES WEBB/PHOTOTAKE.

The infective stage of the hookworm larva.

TAPEWORMS

There are many species of tapeworms. They are carried by fleas! The dog eats the flea and starts the tapeworm cycle. Humans can also be infected with tapeworms, so don't eat fleas! Fleas are so small that your dog could pass them onto your hands, your plate or your food and thus make it possible for you to ingest a flea which is carrying tapeworm eggs.

While tapeworm infection is not life threatening in dogs (smart parasite!), it can be the cause of a very serious liver disease for humans. About 50 percent of the humans infected with

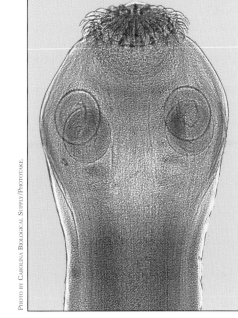

PHOTO BY CAROLINA BIOLOGICAL SUPPLY/PHOTOTAKE.

The head and rostellum (the round prominence on the scolex) of a tapeworm, which infects dogs and humans.

Echinococcus multilocularis, a type of tapeworm that causes alveolar hydatis, perish.

HEARTWORMS

Heartworms are thin, extended worms up to 30 cms (12 ins) long which live in a dog's heart and the major blood vessels surrounding it. Dogs may have up to 200 of these worms. The symptoms may be loss of energy, loss of appetite, coughing, the development of a pot belly and anaemia.

Heartworms are transmitted by mosquitoes. The mosquito drinks the blood of an infected dog and takes in larvae with the blood. The larvae, called microfilaria, develop within the body of the mosquito and are passed on to the next dog bitten after the larvae mature. It takes two to three weeks for the larvae to develop to the infective stage within the body of the mosquito. Dogs should be treated at about six weeks of age, then every six months.

Did You Know?

Humans, rats, squirrels, foxes, coyotes, wolves, mixed breeds of dogs and purebred dogs are all susceptible to tapeworm infection. Except in humans, tapeworms are usually not a fatal infection.

Infected individuals can harbour a thousand parasitic worms.

Tapeworms have two sexes—male and female (many other worms have only one sex—male and female in the same worm).

If dogs eat infected rats or mice, they get the tapeworm disease.

One month after attaching to a dog's intestine, the worm starts shedding eggs. These eggs are infective immediately.

Infective eggs can live for a few months without a host animal.

Roundworms, whipworms and tapeworms are just a few of the other commonly known worms that infect dogs.

Blood testing for heartworms is not necessarily indicative of how seriously your dog is infected. This is a dangerous disease. Although heartworm is a problem for dogs in America, Australia, Asia and Central Europe, dogs in the United Kingdom are not affected by heartworm.

The heartworm, *Dirofilaria immitis*.

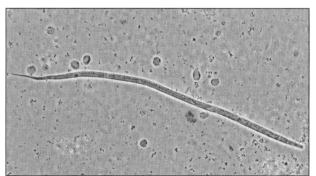

PHOTO BY JAMES E HAYDEN, RPB/PHOTOTAKE

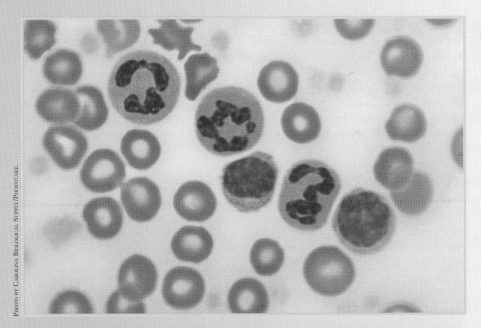

PHOTO BY CAROLINA BIOLOGICAL SUPPLY/PHOTOTAKE.

Magnified heartworm larvae, *Dirofilaria immitis.*

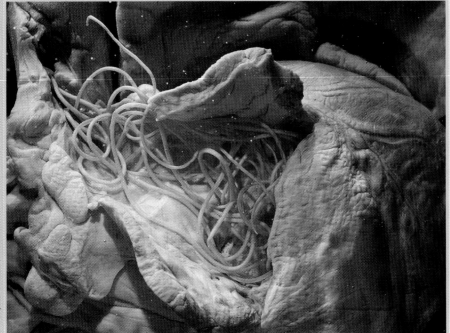

PHOTO BY JAMES E HAYDEN, RPB/PHOTOTAKE.

The heart of a dog infected with canine heartworm, *Dirofilaria immitis.*

135

CDS: COGNITIVE DYSFUNCTION SYNDROME
'Old Dog Syndrome'

There are many ways for you to evaluate old-dog syndrome. Veterinary surgeons have defined CDS (cognitive dysfunction syndrome) as the gradual deterioration of cognitive abilities. These are indicated by changes in the dog's behaviour. When a dog changes its routine response, and maladies have been eliminated as the cause of these behavioural changes, then CDS is the usual diagnosis.

More than half the dogs over 8 years old suffer some form of CDS. The older the dog, the more chance it has of suffering from CDS. In humans, doctors often dismiss the CDS behavioural changes as part of 'winding down.'

There are four major signs of CDS: frequent toilet accidents inside the home, sleeps much more or much less than normal, acts confused, and fails to respond to social stimuli.

SYMPTOMS OF CDS

FREQUENT TOILET ACCIDENTS
- *Urinates in the house.*
- *Defecates in the house.*
- *Doesn't signal that he wants to go out.*

SLEEP PATTERNS
- *Moves much more slowly.*
- *Sleeps more than normal during the day.*
- *Sleeps less during the night.*
- *Walks around listlessly and without a destination goal.*

CONFUSION
- *Goes outside and just stands there.*
- *Appears confused with a faraway look in his eyes.*
- *Hides more often.*
- *Doesn't recognise friends.*
- *Doesn't come when called.*

FAILS TO RESPOND TO SOCIAL STIMULI
- *Comes to people less frequently, whether called or not.*
- *Doesn't tolerate petting for more than a short time.*
- *Doesn't come to the door when you return home from work.*

YOUR SENIOR
CAIRN TERRIER

The term old is a qualitative term. For dogs, as well as their masters, old is relative. Certainly we can all distinguish between a puppy Cairn Terrier and an adult Cairn Terrier—there are the obvious physical traits, such as size, appearance and facial expressions, and personality traits. Puppies that are nasty are very rare. Puppies and young dogs like to play with children. Children's natural exuberance is a good match for the seemingly endless energy of young dogs. They like to run, jump, chase and retrieve. When dogs grow up and cease their interaction with children, they are often thought of as being too old to play with the kids.

On the other hand, if a Cairn Terrier is only exposed to people over 60 years of age, its life will normally be less active and it will not seem to be getting old as its activity level slows down.

If people live to be 100 years old, dogs live to be 20 years old. Whilst this is a good rule of thumb, it is very inaccurate. When trying to compare dog years to human years, you cannot make a generalisation about all dogs. Terriers as a whole are long-lived dogs and your Cairn will be no different. If your dog lives to 8 years of age, he will often last until 12 years of age and sometimes even as long as 16 years of age. Give your dog his yearly inoculations, visit the

This delightful old girl exhibits the tell-tale signs of her senior hears: greying on her coat and a wisdom that is ineffable.

137

Did You Know?

An old dog starts to show one or more of the following symptoms:

• The hair on its face and paws starts to turn grey. The colour breakdown usually starts around the eyes and mouth.

• Sleep patterns are deeper and longer and the old dog is harder to awaken.

• Food intake diminishes.

• Responses to calls, whistles and other signals are ignored more and more.

• Eye contacts do not evoke tail wagging (assuming they once did)

veterinarian as needed, feed him a good diet and give him plenty of exercise and your dog should live a long life with you and give you much pleasure.

Dogs are generally considered mature within three years, but they can reproduce even earlier. So the first three years of a dog's life are like seven times that of comparable humans. That means a 3-year-old dog is like a 21-year-old human. As the curve of comparison shows, there is no hard and fast rule for comparing dog and human ages. The comparison is made even more difficult, for not all humans age at the same rate...and human females live longer than human males.

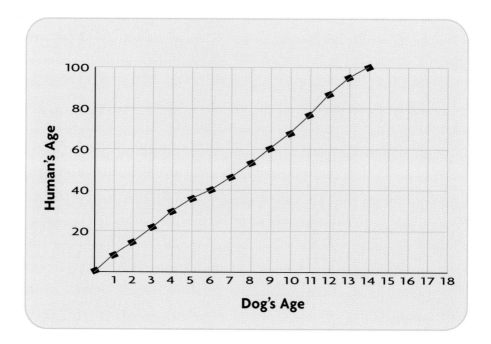

WHAT TO LOOK FOR IN SENIORS

Most veterinary surgeons and behaviourists use the seventh year mark as the time to consider a dog a 'senior.' The term 'senior' does not imply that the dog is geriatric and has begun to fail in mind and body. Ageing is essentially a slowing process. Humans readily admit that they feel a difference in their activity level from age 20 to 30, and then from 30 to 40, etc. By treating the seven-year-old dog as a senior, owners are able to implement certain therapeutic and preventive medical strategies with the help of their veterinary surgeons. A senior-care programme should include at least two veterinary visits per year, screening sessions to determine the dog's health status, as well as nutritional counselling. Veterinary surgeons determine the

A senior male showing his age on his muzzle. Seniors need special attention from their adoring owners. It's time to show your Cairn how important he is to you and your family.

senior dog's health status through a blood smear for a complete blood count, serum chemistry profile with electrolytes, urinalysis, blood pressure check, electrocardiogram, ocular tonometry (pressure on the eyeball), and dental prophylaxis.

Such an extensive programme for senior dogs is well advised before owners start to see the obvious physical signs of ageing, such as slower and inhibited movement, greying, increased sleep/nap periods and disinterest in play and other activity. This preventative programme promises a longer, healthier life for the ageing dog. Amongst the physical problems common in ageing dogs are the loss of sight and hearing,

Did You Know?

The bottom line is simply that a dog is getting old when YOU think it is getting old because it slows down in its general activities, including walking, running, eating, jumping and retrieving. On the other hand, certain activities increase, such as more sleeping, more barking and more repetition of habits like going to the door without being called when you put your coat on to leave or go outdoors.

139

arthritis, kidney and liver failure, diabetes mellitus, heart disease, and Cushing's disease (a hormonal disease).

In addition to the physical manifestations discussed, there are some behavioural changes and problems related to ageing dogs. Dogs suffering from hearing or vision loss, dental discomfort or arthritis can become aggressive. Likewise the near-deaf and/or blind dog may be startled more easily and react in an unexpectedly aggressive manner. Seniors suffering from senility can become more impatient and irritable. Housesoiling accidents are associated with loss of mobility, kidney problems, loss of sphincter control as well as plaque accumulation, physiological brain changes, and reactions to medications. Older dogs, just like young puppies, suffer from separation anxiety, which can lead to excessive barking, whining, housesoiling and destructive behaviour. Seniors may become fearful of everyday sounds, such as vacuum cleaners, heaters, thunder and passing traffic. Some dogs have difficulty sleeping, due to discomfort, the need for frequent potty visits and the like. Owners should avoid spoiling the older dog with too many fatty treats. Obesity is a common problem in older dogs and subtracts years from their lifespan. Keep the senior dog as trim as possible since excessive weight puts additional stress on the body's vital organs. Some breeders recommend supplementing the diet with foods high in fibre and lower in calories. Adding fresh vegetables and marrow broth to the senior's diet makes a tasty, low-calorie, low-fat supplement. Vets also offer specialty diets for senior dogs that are worth exploring.

Your dog, as he nears his twilight years, needs his owner's patience and good care more than ever. Never punish an older dog for

Did You Know?

The symptoms listed below are symptoms that gradually appear and become more noticeable. They are not life threatening; however, the symptoms below are to be taken very seriously and a discussion with your veterinary surgeon is warranted:

• Your dog cries and whimpers when it moves and stops running completely.

• Convulsions start or become more serious and frequent. The usual convulsion (spasm) is when the dog stiffens and starts to tremble being unable or unwilling to move. The seizure usually lasts for 5 to 30 minutes.

• Your dog drinks more water and urinates more frequently. Wetting and bowel accidents take place indoors without warning.

• Vomiting becomes more and more frequent.

an accident or abnormal behaviour. For all the years of love, protection and companionship that your dog has provided, he deserves special attention and courtesies. The older dog may need to relieve himself at 3 a.m. because he can no longer hold it for eight hours. Older dogs may not be able to remain crated for more than two or three hours. It may be time to give up a sofa or chair to your old friend. Although he may not seem as enthusiastic about your attention and petting, he does appreciate the considerations you offer as he gets older.

Your Cairn Terrier does not understand why his world is slowing down. Owners must make the transition into the golden years as pleasant and rewarding as possible.

WHAT TO DO WHEN THE TIME COMES

You are never fully prepared to make a rational decision about putting your dog to sleep. It is very obvious that you love your Cairn Terrier or you would not be reading this book. Putting a loved dog to sleep is extremely difficult. It is a decision that must be made with your veterinary surgeon. You are usually forced to make the decision when one of the life-threatening symptoms listed above becomes serious enough for you to seek medical (veterinary) help.

If the prognosis of the malady indicates the end is near and your beloved pet will only suffer more and experience no enjoyment for the balance of its life, then euthanasia is the right choice.

WHAT IS EUTHANASIA?

Euthanasia derives from the Greek meaning *good death*. In other words, it means the planned, painless killing of a dog suffering from a painful, incurable condition, or who is so aged that it cannot walk, see, eat or control its excretory functions.

Euthanasia is usually accomplished by injection with an overdose of an anaesthesia or barbiturate. Aside from the prick of the needle, the experience is usually painless.

How About You?

The decision to euthanise your dog is never easy. The days during which the dog becomes ill and the end occurs can be unusually stressful for you. If this is your first experience with the death of a loved one, you may need the comfort dictated by your religious beliefs. If you are the head of the family and have children, you should have involved them in the

Most pet cemeteries have a suitable resting place for your dog's ashes.

decision of putting your Cairn Terrier to sleep. Usually your dog can be maintained on drugs for a few days in order to give you ample time to make a decision. During this time, talking with members of your family or even people who have lived through this same experience can ease the burden of your inevitable decision.

The Final Resting Place

Dogs can have some of the same privileges as humans. They can occasionally be buried in their entirety in a pet cemetery which is generally expensive, or if they have died at home can be buried in your garden in a place suitably marked with some stone or newly planted tree or bush. Alternatively they can be cremated and the ashes returned to you, or some people prefer to leave their dogs at the surgery for the vet to dispose of.

All of these options should be discussed frankly and openly with your veterinary surgeon. Do not be afraid to ask financial questions. Cremations can be individual, but a less expensive option is mass cremation, although of course the ashes can not then be returned. Vets can usually arrange cremation services on your behalf, but you must be aware that in Britain if your dog has died at the surgery the vet cannot legally allow you to take your dog's body home.

Getting Another Dog?

The grief of losing your beloved dog will be as lasting as the grief of losing a human friend or relative. You cannot go out and buy another grandfather, but you can go out and buy another Cairn Terrier. In most cases, if your dog died of old age (if there is such a thing), it had slowed down considerably. Do you want a new Cairn Terrier puppy to replace it? Or are you better off in finding a more mature Cairn

Views at a typical cemetery for pets. Many cemeteries have a perpetual care plan.

Terrier, say two to three years of age, which will usually be housetrained and will have an already developed personality. In this case, you can find out if you like each other after a few hours of being together.

The decision is, of course, your own. Do you want another Cairn Terrier or perhaps a different breed so as to avoid comparison with your beloved friend?. Most people usually buy the same breed because they know (and love) the characteristics of that breed. Then, too, they often know people who have the same breed and perhaps they are lucky enough that one of their friends expects a litter soon. What could be better?

143

When you purchased your Cairn Terrier you will have made it clear to the breeder whether you wanted one just as a loveable companion and pet, or if you hoped to be buying a Cairn Terrier with show prospects. No reputable breeder will have sold you a young puppy saying that it was definitely of show quality for so much can go wrong during the early weeks and months of a puppy's development. If you plan to show what you will hopefully have acquired is a puppy with 'show potential.'

To the novice, exhibiting a Cairn Terrier in the show ring may look easy but it usually takes a lot of hard work and devotion to do top winning at a show such as the prestigious Crufts, not to mention a little luck too!

The first concept that the canine novice learns when watching a dog show is that each breed first competes against members of its own breed. Once the judge has selected the best member of each breed, provided that the show is judged on a Group system, that chosen dog will compete with other dogs in its group. Finally the best of each group will compete for Best in Show and Reserve Best in Show.

The second concept that you must understand is that the dogs are not actually compared against one another. The judge compares each dog against the breed standard, which is a written description of the ideal specimen of the breed. Whilst some early breed standards were indeed based on specific dogs that were famous or popular, many dedicated enthusiasts say that a perfect specimen, described in the standard, has never been bred. Thus the 'perfect' dog never walked into a show ring, has never been bred and, to the woe of dog breeders around the globe, does not exist. Breeders attempt to get as close to this ideal as possible, with every litter, but

Did You Know?

The Kennel Club divides its dogs into seven Groups: Gundogs, Utility, Working, Toy, Terrier, Hounds and Pastoral.*

*The Pastoral Group, established in 1999, includes those sheepdog breeds previously categorised in the Working Group.

theoretically the 'perfect' dog is so elusive that it is impossible. (And if the 'perfect' dog were born, breeders and judges would never agree that it was indeed 'perfect.')

If you are interested in exploring dog shows, your best bet is to join your local breed club. These clubs often host both Championship and Open shows, and sometimes Match meetings and Special Events, all of which could be of interest, even if you are only an onlooker. Clubs also send out newsletters and some organise training days and seminars in order that people may learn more about their chosen breed. To locate the nearest breed club for you, contact The Kennel Club, the ruling body for the British dog world. The Kennel Club governs not only conforma-tion shows but also working trials, obedience trials, agility trials and field trials. The Kennel Club furnishes the rules and regulations for all these events plus general

Winning The Ticket

Earning a championship at Kennel Club shows is the most difficult in the world. Compared to the United States and Canada where it is relatively not 'challenging,' collecting three green tickets not only requires much time and effort, it can be very expensive! Challenge Certificates, as the tickets are properly known, are the building blocks of champions—good breeding, good handling, good training and good luck!

145

The world's oldest dog show is the Westminster Kennel Club Dog Show, which takes place annually in New York City. The group finals are completely televised, and the show has an attendance of more than 50,000 people per day.

This pair of Cairn Terriers took Best of All-Breeds, Couples, in Holland in 1997.

dog registration and other basic requirements of dog ownership. Its annual show called the Crufts Dogs Show, held in Birmingham, is the largest bench show in England. Every year around 20,000 of the U.K.'s best dogs qualify to participate in this marvellous show which lasts four days.

Show Ring Etiquette

Showing your dog can be quite intimidating to you as a novice when it seems as if everyone else knows what they are doing. You can familiarise yourself with ring procedure beforehand by taking a class to prepare you and your dog for conformation showing or by talking with an experienced handler. When you are in the ring, listen and pay attention to the judge and follow his/her directions. Remember, even the most skilled handlers had to start somewhere. Keep it up and you too will become a proficient handler before too long!

The Kennel Club governs many different kinds of shows. At the most competitive and prestigious of these shows, the Championship Shows, a dog can earn Challenge Certificates, and thereby become a Show Champion or a Champion. A dog must earn three Challenge Certificates under three different judges to earn the prefix of 'Sh Ch' or 'Ch.' Note that some breeds must also qualify in a field trial in order to gain the title of full champion. Challenge Certificates are awarded to a very small percentage of the dogs competing, especially as dogs which are already Champions compete with others for these coveted CCs. The number of Challenge Certificates awarded in any one year is based upon the total number of dogs in each breed entered for competition. There are three types of Championship Shows: an all-breed General Championship show for all-Kennel-Club-recognised breeds; a Group Championship Show, limited to breeds within one of the Groups; and a Breed Show, usually confined to a single breed. The Kennel Club determines which breeds at which Championship Shows will have the opportunity to earn Challenge Certificates (or tickets). Serious exhibitors often will opt not to participate if the tickets are withheld at a particular show. This policy makes earning championships even more difficult to accomplish.

Open Shows are generally less competitive and are frequently used as 'practice shows' for young dogs. There are hundreds of Open Shows each year that can be invitingly social events and are great first show experiences for the novice. Even if you're considering just watching a show to wet your paws, an Open Show is a great choice.

Whilst Championship and Open Shows are most important for the beginner to understand, there are other types of shows in which the interested dog owner can participate. Training clubs sponsor Matches that can be entered on the day of the show for a nominal fee. In these introductory-level exhibitions, two dogs are pulled out of a hat and 'matched,' the winner of that match goes on to the next round, and eventually only one dog is left undefeated.

Classes at Dog Shows

There can be as many as 18 classes per sex for your breed. Check the show schedule carefully to make sure that you have entered your dog in the appropriate class. Among the classes offered can be: Beginners; Minor Puppy (ages 6 to 9 months); Puppy (ages 6 to 12 months); Junior (ages 6 to 18 months); Beginners (handler or dog never won first place) as well as the following, each of which is defined in the schedule: Maiden; Novice; Tyro; Debutant; Undergraduate; Graduate; Postgraduate; Minor Limit; Mid Limit; Limit; Open; Veteran; Stud Dog; Brood Bitch; Progeny; Brace and Team.

Exemption Shows are much more light-hearted affairs with usually only four pedigree classes and several 'fun' classes, all of which can be entered on the day. The proceeds of an Exemption Show must be given to a charity and are sometimes held in conjunction with small agricultural shows. Limited Shows are also available in small number, but entry is restricted to members of the club which hosts the show, although one can usually join the club when making an entry.

Before you actually step into the ring, you would be well advised to sit back and observe the judge's ring procedure. If it is your first time in the ring, do not be over-anxious and run to the front of the line. It is much better to stand back and study how the exhibitor in front of you is performing. The judge asks each

handler to 'stand' the dog, hopefully showing the dog off to his best advantage. The judge will observe the dog from a distance and from different angles, approach the dog, check his teeth, overall structure, alertness and muscle tone, as well as consider how well the dog 'conforms' to the standard. Most importantly, the judge will have the exhibitor move the dog around the ring in some pattern that he or she should specify (another advantage to not going first, but always listen since some judges change their directions, and the judge is always

How to Enter a Dog Show

1. Obtain an entry form and show schedule from the Show Secretary.
2. Select the classes that you want to enter and complete the entry form.
3. Transfer your dog into your name at The Kennel Club. (Be sure that this matter is handled before entering.)
4. Find out how far in advance show entries must be made. Oftentimes it's more than a couple of months.

The handler must be attentive to the judge's wishes during the physical examination. Your Cairn must be trained to tolerate the handling of a stranger in order to compete in a dog show.

Did You Know?

You can get information about dog shows from kennel clubs and breed clubs:

Fédération Cynologique Internationale
14, rue Leopold II, B-6530 Thuin, Belgium
www.fci.be

The Kennel Club
1-5 Clarges St., Piccadilly, London
W1Y 8AB, UK
www.the-kennel-club.org.uk

American Kennel Club
5580 Centerview Dr., Raleigh, NC
27606-3390, USA
www.akc.org

Canadian Kennel Club
89 Skyway Ave., Suite 100
Etobicoke, Ontario
M9W 6R4 Canada
www.ckc.ca

This young Cairn is being exhibited for the first time in the ring. It is unusual that a young dog will do well, so don't be disheartened if you are not selected at your very first show.

151

right!) Finally the judge will give the dog one last look before moving on to the next exhibitor.

If you are not in the top three at your first show, do not be discouraged. Be patient and consistent and you may eventually find yourself in the winning lineup. Remember that the winners were once in your shoes and have devoted many hours and much money to earn the placement. If you find that your dog is losing every time and never getting a nod, it may be time to consider a different dog sport or just enjoy your Cairn Terrier as a pet.

Did You Know?

FCI-recognised breeds are divided into ten Groups:
Group 1: Sheepdogs and Cattle-dogs (except Swiss Cattledogs)
Group 2: Pinschers and Schnau-zers, Molossians, Swiss Mountain Dogs and Swiss Cattledogs
Group 3: Terriers
Group 4: Dachshunds
Group 5: Spitz- and primitive-type dogs
Group 6: Scenthounds and related breeds
Group 7: Pointing dogs
Group 8: Retrievers, Flushing dogs and Water dogs
Group 9: Companion and Toy dogs
Group 10: Sighthounds

WORKING TRIALS

Working trials can be entered by any well-trained dog of any breed, not just Gundogs or Working dogs. Many dogs that earn the Kennel Club Good Citizen Dog award choose to participate in a working trial. There are five stakes at both open and championship levels: Companion Dog (CD), Utility Dog (UD), Working Dog (WD), Tracking Dog (TD) and Patrol Dog (PD). As in conformation shows, dogs compete against a

standard and if the dog reaches the qualifying mark, it obtains a certificate. Divided into groups, each exercise must be achieved 70 percent in order to qualify. If the dog achieves 80 percent in the open level, it receives a Certificate of Merit (COM), in the championship level, it receives a Qualifying Certificate. At the CD stake, dogs must participate in four groups, Control, Stay, Agility and Search (Retrieve and Nosework). At the next three levels, UD, WD and TD, there are only three groups: Control, Agility and Nosework.

Agility consists of three jumps: a vertical scale up a wall of planks; a clear jump over a basic hurdle with a removable top bar; and a long jump across angled planks.

To earn the UD, WD and TD, dogs must track approximately one-half mile for articles laid from one-half hour to three hours ago. Tracks consist of turns and legs, and fresh ground is used for each participant.

The fifth stake, PD, involves teaching manwork, which is not recommended for every breed.

This is what its all about...winning! This dog took Best of Breed, proving that he was the best Cairn Terrier entered that day.

Did You Know?

There are 329 breeds recognised by the FCI, and each breed is considered to be 'owned' by a specific country. Each breed standard is a cooperative effort between the breed's country and the FCI's Standards and Scientific Commissions. Judges use these official breed standards at shows held in FCI member countries. One of the functions of the FCI is to update and translate the breed standards into French, English, Spanish and German.

FIELD TRIALS AND WORKING TESTS

Working tests are frequently used to prepare dogs for field trials, the purpose of which is to heighten the instincts and natural abilities of gundogs. Live game is not used in working tests. Unlike field trials, working tests do not count toward a dog's record at The Kennel Club, though the same judges often oversee working tests. Field trials began in England in 1947 and are only moderately popular amongst dog folk. Whilst breeders of Working and Gundog breeds concern themselves with the field abilities of their dogs, there is considerably less interest in field trials than dog shows. In order for dogs to become full champions, certain breeds must qualify in the field as well. Upon gaining three CCs in the show ring, the dog is designated a Show Champion (Sh Ch). The title Champion (Ch) requires that the dog gain an award at a field trial, be a 'special qualifier' at a field trial or pass a 'special show dog qualifier' judged by a field trial judge on a shooting day.

AGILITY TRIALS

Agility trials began in the United Kingdom in 1977 and have since spread around the world, especially to the United States, where it enjoys strong popularity. The handler directs his dog over an obstacle course that includes jumps (such as those used in the

working trials), as well as tyres, the dog walk, weave poles, pipe tunnels, collapsed tunnels, etc. The Kennel Club requires that dogs not be trained for agility until they are 12 months old. This dog sport intends to be great fun for dog and owner and interested owners should join a training club that has obstacles and experienced agility handlers who can introduce you and your dog to the 'ropes' (and tyres, tunnels and so on).

FÉDÉRATION CYNOLOGIQUE INTERNATIONALE

Established in 1911, the Fédération Cynologique Internationale (FCI) represents the 'world kennel

club.' This international body brings uniformity to the breeding, judging and showing of purebred dogs. Although the FCI originally included only four European nations: France, Holland, Austria and Belgium (which remains its headquarters), the organisation today embraces nations on six continents and recognises well over 300 breeds of purebred dog. There are three titles attainable through the FCI: the International Champion, which is the most prestigious; the International Beauty Champion, which is based on aptitude certificates in different countries; and the International Trial Champion, which is based on achievement in obedience trials in different countries. Quarantine laws in England and Australia prohibit most of their exhibitors from entering FCI shows. The rest of the Continent does participate in these impressive canine spectacles, the largest of which is the World Dog Show, hosted in a different country each year. FCI sponsors both national and international shows. The hosting country determines the judging system and breed standards are always based on the breed's country of origin.

The FCI is divided into ten 'Groups.' At the World Dog Show, the following 'Classes' are offered for each breed: Puppy Class (6–9 months), Youth Class (9–18 months), Open Class (15 months or older) and Champion Class. A dog can be awarded a classification of Excellent, Very Good, Good, Sufficient and Not Sufficient. Puppies can be awarded classifications of Very Promising, Promising or Not Promising. Four placements are made in each class. After all sexes and classes are judged, a Best of Breed is selected. Other special groups and classes may also be shown. Each exhibitor showing a dog receives a written evaluation from the judge.

Besides the World Dog Show, you can exhibit your dog at speciality shows held by different breed clubs. Speciality shows may have their own regulations.

The Cairn Terrier won second in the Group at the famous Crufts Show in 1999. Winning the Group was a Norwich Terrier.

INDEX

Page numbers in boldface indicate illustrations.

Adult diets 64
Age 85
Agility trials 103, 153-154
Allergies
—airborne 116
—food 117
America 16
American Kennel Club 16, 18
—address 151
American Working Terrier Association 22
Ancylostoma caninum **132**
Arlen, Harold 21
Ascaris lumbricoides **132**
Axelrod, Dr Herbert R 131
Backpacking 103
Bathing 72
Bedding 42
Benyon, J W 10
Bhan, Cuillean 12
Bite 37
Blencathra Kennels 15
Boarding 78
Bones 45
Bonfire of Twobees 14
Bowls 47
Bradshaw, Walter 14
Breed standard 26, 144
Breeder 32-33, 36
Brocaire Kennels 12
Burial 142
Cairmar Kennels 18
Cairn 10
Cairn Terrier Club of America 18
Cairndainia Kennels 15, 18
Cairnwoods Golden Boy 18
Cairnwoods Quince 14
Caithness Kennels 17
Caithness Rufus 17
Calla Mhor 14
Campbell, Alastair 12

Canadian Kennel Club
—address 151
Cars 76
Cat 93
CDS 136
Cerebellar hypoplasia 24
Certificate of Gameness 22
Challenge Certificates 13, 145, 148
Champion 148, 154
Championship Shows 148
Chewing 88
Cheyletiella 129
Choke collars 47
Coat 68
Cognitive dysfunction syndrome 136
Collar 47, 93
Colostrum 63
Come 98
Commands 95
Congenital disorders 23
Coronavirus 112
Craniomandibular osteopathy 24
Crate 41, 60, 76, 87, 89
—training 89
Crufts Dogs Show 148
Crying 59
Ctenocephalides **122**
Ctenocephalides canis **122, 125**
Ctenocephalides felis **125**
Cushing's disease 108
Demodex 129
Dermacentor variabilis **129**
Destructive behaviour 140
Development schedule 85
Deworming programme 131
Diet
—adult 64
—puppy 62
—senior 65
Dirofilaria immitis **134-135**
Discipline 92

Distemper 112
Dog flea 122, 125
Dog tick 129
Doughall Out of the West 13
Down 96
Ear cleaning 73
Echinococcus multilocularis **134**
Emerald City, The 21
Euthanasia 141
Exemption Shows 150
Exercise 66
External parasites 122
Family introduction to pup 51
FCI 154
Fear period 54
Fédération Cynologique Internationale 154
—address 151
Fence 50
Field trials 154
First aid 107
Fisherman Out of the West 13
Flea 122, 126
—life cycle **124**
Fleig, Dr Dieter 12
Fleming, N 13
Food 62
—allergy 117
—intolerance 117
—treats 102
Garland, Judy 21
Gender 35
Globoid-cell leukodystrophy 24
Good Citizen Dog award 152
Grooming 23, 66
Handling 150
Harviestoun Raider 13
Heartworm 134-135
Heel 100
Hemophilia 25
Hepatitis 112
Hip dysplasia 25
History of Fighting Dogs 12
Home preparation 40
Hookworm 132
—larva 133
Housebreaking 83

—schedule 89
Hyslop, Betty 15, 18
Identification 79
Inguinal hernias 25
Inhalant allergies 25
Internal parasites 131
Isle of Skye 11
Ixode 129
Judge 150
Kennel Club, The 12, 14, 18, 26, 33, 144-145
—address 151
Kennel cough 112
Kerr, J E 13
Kilbride 11
Killybracken Kennels 17
Krabbe's disease 24
Kuhn, Dwight R. 126
Lead 45, 93
Leighton, Robert 13
Leptospirosis 112
Lice **126**
Life expectancy 137
Limited Shows 150
Lofthouse Kennels 16
Lord Hawke 13
Lupus 116
Mac Leod, Captain 11
Mange 129
—mite 130
Manley, H L 16
Matches 149
Mhor, Calla 12
Mhor, Rog 12
Milk 63
Mites 129
—infestation 73
Myasthenia gravis 25
Nail clipping 74
Neutering 112
Nipping 59
Obedience 22
Obedience class 80, 102
Obesity 66, 140
Old dog syndrome 136
Open Shows 149
Oudenarde Kennels 16

Oudenarde Sea Hark 16
Out of the West Kennels 13, 16
Ownership 37
Panleukopenia 24
Parasites
—bites 116
—external 122
—internal 131
Parvovirus 112
Pollen allergy 116
Price, Mrs Henry 16
Prick-eared Skye Terriers 12
Psoroptes bovis **130**
Punishment 92
Puppy
—food 62
—health 108
—problems 54, 58
—selection 35
—training 81
Puppy-Proofing 48
Rabies 112
Rat fights 12
Redletter Elford Mhorag 15
Redletter Kennels 14
Redletter Marcel 15
Redletter Mc Bryan 15
Redletter Mc Joe 15
Redletter Mc Murran 15
Redletter Mc Ruffie 19
Redletter My Choice 14
Redletter Twinlaw Seaspirit 15
Rhabditis **131-132**
Rhipicephalus sanguineus **129**
Roundworm 131-132
Sandy Peter Out of the West 16
Scottish Kennel Club 12
Scottish Terrier 10, **11**
Senior 139
—diets 65
Separation anxiety 60, 140
Sex 35
Shagbark Kennel 17
Short-haired Skye Terrier 11, 13
Show Champion 148, 154
Sit 95
Skin problems 115

—inherited 115
Skye Terrier 10, **11**
Socialisation 33, 54
Splinter of Twobees 14
Sport of Zellah 14
Standard 26, 144
Stay 97
Stone, Betty 17
Stripping 69
Tam Glen of Killybracken 17
Tapeworm 131, 133
Temperament 33, 35
Terra 9
Therapy dogs 23
Thorndike's Theory of Learning 92
Thorndike, Dr Edward 92
Tickets 148
Ticks 129
Tod-hunter 11
Toptwig Kennels 16
Toto 21
Toxocara canis **131**
Toys 43
Tracheobronchitis 112
Training equipment 93
Travelling 76
Treats 93
Type 10
Uncinaria stenocephala 132
Uniquecottage Kennels 16
Vaccinations 109
Veterinary surgeon 50, 105-106, 127, 131
Water 66
Watermist 11, 13
West Highland White Terrier **10, 18**
Westminster Kennel Club 19
Whining 59
Wolfpit Kennels 18
Wonderful Wizard of Oz 21
Working tests 154
Working trials 152
World Dog Show 155

My Cairn Terrier

PUT YOUR PUPPY'S FIRST PICTURE HERE

Dog's Name _____

Date _____ Photographer _____